CONFIDENTIAL CHATS WITH GIRLS

This edition published by Lector House in 2024

ISBN: 978-93-6138-957-3

Lector House LLP
Registered Office: H. No. 96, Block C, Tomar Colony,
Burari, Delhi – 110084, India
info@lectorhouse.com
www.lectorhouse.com

CONFIDENTIAL CHATS WITH GIRLS

WILLIAM LEE HOWARD

2024

LECTOR HOUSE LLP

CONFIDENTIAL CHATS WITH GIRLS

BY

WILLIAM LEE HOWARD, M.D.

Author of
"Plain Facts on Sex Hygiene," "Confidential Chats with Boys,"
"Facts for the Married"

Foreword

The American girl from fourteen to eighteen years of age has been sadly neglected in the most important and necessary part of her education.

Knowledge of unessentials and nursery physiology, along with a smattering of academic teachings, have held her apart from a true appreciation of her real value to herself and humanity. Physical exercise and moral admonition have been given her, but not advice nor instruction which was based upon the proper foundation—sex development.

Details of sex hygiene have been kept from her, and these, with the care of woman's greatest jewel, maternal possibilities through a perfect sex growth, have all been left to chance and too often sad experience.

The girl is no longer completely protected by the old home influences. To-day she is out in the world alone, struggling for herself and frequently for others. The high-school girl seems to be left in the same whirlpool of moving men and things, and just now there are unpleasant revelations of the fact that she needs care and instruction more than her working sisters.

I have seen in private and hospital practice thousands of girls whose health was ruined for life through ignorance or false ideas concerning sex activities. The land is crowded with suffering wives and broken-down girls whose woeful conditions are due entirely to ignorance of sex hygiene and how to mentally and physically care for their sex development.

If I can, by my humble efforts, stop the future mothers from suffering, worry and ill health, from bringing their daughters up in a state of criminal prudery, I shall be proof against the slings and arrows of the fast-disappearing SHAM.

In these CONFIDENTIAL CHATS I tell in plain language and facts the things that, had they been told to the girls of the last generation, would have saved untold misery.

It is a pity that the facts and instruction which should come from a mother and a father (due quite largely to their own ignorance), must be sought elsewhere, but this being so, I intend that these Chats shall supply what prudery and ignorance have denied the girls of to-day. WILLIAM LEE HOWARD, M.D.

Contents

Chapter		*Page*
I.	How to Develop into Womanhood	1
II.	A General Chat	8
III.	The Disorders of Menstruation and General Health	19
IV.	The Care of the Skin and Complexion	31
V.	Nerves and the Nervous Girl	46
VI.	How to Get Will Power	54
VII.	How to Keep Attractive	60
VIII.	Some Don'ts.	70

CONFIDENTIAL CHATS WITH GIRLS

Chapter I

How to Develop into Womanhood

The little buds on the rosebushes seen in the warm spring days and which later on in the early summer open to become the beautiful flowers, are controlled and governed in their development by the same laws of Nature that control your development from the little girl to a budding girl, and then into the full blossoming woman.

Every living thing upon this earth is given life, growth and development under laws that are the same for the girl, the woman, the flowers, the fishes, the little birds. The supreme Power which controls us and every living being has so regulated the way man, beasts, birds, fishes and even flowers are kept on the earth for the increase and progression of the world, that by a plain understanding of these laws we can live and produce better and better men and women from generation to generation.

If you will carefully think the matter over, you will soon realize that every living thing around us is the result of the mating of the male with the female. Roses marry and have little children just the same as a man and woman. The little pussy willow, which so early in the spring sends out its little babies in furry buds, had been married to a willow man the year before. The sweet grapes you eat in the autumn are the "fruit of the marriage" between a male grape and a female grape—that is, the seeds. The little chicks hovering and hiding around the proud mother hen have for their father the crowing cock.

Here is a good example of this absolute law of the supreme Power. If you take a few chickens, all females, and keep them shut up until they are young hens with no rooster ever disturbing their happiness, you can never hatch chicks from the eggs of these hens. You may put these eggs under a setting hen and she may sit there until the hens' doomsday and no life is possible in these eggs. Now at the same time shut up chickens with a rooster, and when these chickens have grown to be hens you will be able to hatch chicks from their eggs. If you take the eggs from your first lot of hens and in a dark room examine their eggs, by the aid of a candle, you will see only a clear egg. Now if you take an egg from the lot of hens who have had the rooster for companionship and hold it up to a candle, in a dark room, you will be able to see a tiny black or brown spot about the size of a pin's head. This is the vital spot, the male seed which, upon entering the vital principle of the female egg, at once begins to develop into a chick. Three weeks under the warm body of the setting hen causes the development of the chick from this tiny spot.

The little black spots you see in a mass of "frog spittle" are the vitalizing—the life-giving—seed from the bullfrog. These male seeds lie in the mass thrown out by the female frog. Placed in some quiet pool of warm water, warmed by the sun, the hatching goes on until the pollywogs are born. It is the same with the fishes, the turtles—every living thing—the male seed must enter the eggs of the female before life commences. The playful puppies, the fuzzy kittens, the butterflies, the bees are all brought to life by the same principle.

Always keep in your mind that no matter what the different ways of mating are, how the little flower children are born, how the puppies grow before birth and then come into the world; they all are God's creations and made according to His laws. So being made according to God's laws, and we as human beings having absolutely nothing to do with these laws, but are controlled by them, there can be nothing wrong, indelicate or shameful in knowing all about these matters.

In fact, before we can have full reverence for God and obey His laws, we must understand and know them, what they mean to us, how we are punished and warned for disobeying these laws and the fearful results following the abuse of our bodies and minds through ignorance of what our bodies require and God demands.

As I have told you, every living thing, from flowers up to babies, is produced by the meeting of the male seed with that of the female seed. Every female, flower or woman, has a place to keep and hold these seeds until they have grown to be babies of some kind.

Take the roses for example. When the big rose gets fully grown in the latter part of the summer, the little yellow dust you see in the center is the male seed. Botanists call these male flower seeds the pollen. At about the same time that the male rose is "going to seed" the female rose is ready to take this pollen into her receptacle. This male seed is carried to the female rose's womb, the name of the organ in all females where the two kinds of seed meet and then grow into children.

The seed is carried into the rose's womb by the wind, insects and birds. When it is once deposited, the rose's womb closes tightly, and there the seeds of the two sexes remain and grow until in the spring you see the little babies in the buds. These gradually grow, as you know, from the little colorless buds to the small pink ones, and when the warm summer-time comes they burst open to become full-grown male or female flowers, and in the autumn these marry and the next spring become fathers and mothers themselves.

It is the same throughout all Nature. Nothing can become a living thing except through a marriage of the male with the female.

Let us take the little birds for another example. This will show you how the young bird comes from an egg and is born almost the same way that you and I were born—coming from an egg—for this is just what did occur in our case.

The female birds, and all female animals, have what we call ovaries, from the Latin *ovum*, meaning egg. These ovaries are placed, in the birds and all animals, in the deep region of the groin, above the womb in the animals which keep the eggs inside of themselves until the babies are born. Of course, the birds, fishes and all their kind, do not have a real womb, for the eggs are laid outside of their bodies in a nest of some kind. This nest outside corresponds to the nest—the womb—inside of the higher animals.

All eggs are formed in the ovaries; this is what the ovaries are for, and at first they are tiny little spots seen only through a microscope. At certain times, like the mating time of the birds, these eggs drop down from the ovaries, ready to meet the male seed. When this is accomplished the eggs at once begin to put on their shells, which, of course, are only to protect the little growing birds while the mother sits upon the eggs. As soon as the shell is formed the eggs are deposited in the nest, and here the patient mother sits and waits for the little ones to grow until ready to come out and see the wide world.

Then comes the pretty sight of the mother and father flying back and forth from the nest, carrying some big worm or bug to feed the hungry and crying babies. Both father and mother work like Trojans to keep the stomachs of their little children filled, and if you will watch a pair of robins trying to feed their nestful of children, you will say that they are the greediest little things you ever saw.

And they have to be kept crammed with worms and bugs, because their growth is rapid and they must get strength enough to fly and take care of themselves before cold weather comes and to get away from cats, snakes and other animals which want them for food.

And is it not a wonderful fact to contemplate when we know that these little birds will fly a thousand miles to a warm climate for the winter, and will fly the thousand miles on their return in the spring and find their old tree, limb and identical spot where their old home was? If these little birds are watched over by such wonderful laws, what must be the care, laws and rules by which we are governed?

As the little birds come from a shell, after being developed through the warmth of the mother's body, just so do we, after lying in our mother's nest—the womb—come to be born, after we have been warmed and developed for nine months. So you see that what I said about the laws of God being the same for every living thing is the absolute truth.

The Springtime of the girl is when she commences to have her eggs form in the ovaries and drop into her womb. She commences to bud at about the age of fourteen years, and like the delicate buds of the flowers, if care is not taken to protect her growth, ill-health follows and she may so ruin herself that, when she marries, she is unable to be a mother.

While it takes only one spring and summer to make a full-grown flower, or even a robin, the girl needs twelve or fifteen years after she is born to get into her budding age. And her future health, morals and happiness all depend upon how the first four or five years of the budding age is lived. And to live so that she will reach the highest development of woman, the girl must understand all the laws of God and live according to these laws.

It is my purpose in these Chats to show you these laws, as well as to plainly point out to you how man and woman have constantly been disobeying God's words and how we are suffering in consequence of our ignorance and disobedience.

Your ovaries are in place when you are born. Of course they are tiny things and not developed. They remain inactive for many years after you are born. But at about ten years of age the blood commences to flow through them and they gradually develop, like the flower buds, until they reach their ripeness. Of course this development varies in different girls according to their nationality; those from the southern countries developing earlier than those from a more rigid climate. About fourteen years of age is the average age in this country.

When the ovaries are developed the womb has also grown, so that every month it gets rid of blood that accumulates there. But at this period the womb is a very tender organ, delicate, not fully fastened to the ligaments from which it hangs, and any rough play, strain or carelessness at the time of menstruation may ruin you for life.

Every girl should be proud of this budding process and care for it with a heart full of thankfulness. Just see how the little budding trees and flowers are cared for by a good gardener, how careful he is to assist Nature, how by this reverence and thought the wild flowers are brought under cultivation and by the means of the pure soil in which they are planted, by protecting them from frost and harsh treatment, what beautiful blossoms, scents and radiance results.

The laws of God make the wonderful growth and development possible, but man, by acknowledging these laws and abiding by them, is able to increase the beauty and usefulness of all growths.

It is just so with us. If we acknowledge the beneficent order which controls us, if we reverently study to understand God's intentions, then we are aided in all we do to perfect our own development, moral beauty and health. The reward we receive is in having children follow us who have benefited by our reverential and knowing efforts. It is only by such an attitude towards Nature that we progress. Shame of our God-given gifts, studied ignorance of all His laws, the ignoring of our powers for reproducing our kind, all mean a going backwards in civilization. Disease, sin and debasement is certain to follow, and does follow, for most of the misery, disease and poverty is due to our past attitude in ignoring the details of the blossoming period of girls, by allowing the process to go on, paying no attention to the soil—associations and environments—of either the girl or the boy.

Everything in nature moves in cycles—that is, moves in regular periods. The stars, the planets, the sun, the earth, the moon, the tides, the seasons, all go and return at certain fixed intervals. Growths of all kinds on this earth have their periods of birth, development, death. The active periods of every living thing is taken up with reproductive occurrences, or the getting ready for reproduction. The female dog has her regular periods when she is ready to be a happy mother, so do the pretty deer, the squirrels, the fishes, everything. When the fishes' regular period comes around in the spring, we call it the spawning time, with the birds the pretty name of mating. With the woman we call it the menstrual period, from the Latin word meaning monthly.

A pure, honest woman, honest to herself and her God, can see nothing but a wonderful provision of God for keeping the earth populated and the opportunities for bringing man to a nearer understanding of his Maker.

We need no orthodox religion to make man feel the essence of God within him when he understands the laws under which he lives, and how by his own efforts he can improve his powers and give greater ones to those who have received his blood through a pure woman.

Such is every good and intelligent man's thoughts, his inner feelings, but only through a woman's understanding of her greater powers in this respect can we hope to bring future generations to a higher plane.

It is in order to aid you in avoiding the many illnesses which have fastened upon women during the last thirty years or so, that I speak so plainly in these Chats. I am obliged to say things and use words that at first may seem a little indelicate, but if you have grasped the fact that I am humbly trying to tell you the truth about God's laws and sincerely believe that I am doing right in so telling you, there will be no misunderstanding about my motives.

So I shall take you at once into my confidence and let you be the judge.

Chapter II
A General Chat

The average American girl approaches puberty without any definite knowledge of what a menstrual flow means. If you are one of these neglected girls and have had a fright when you first menstruated, had all kinds of stories put into your head, you must try to forget the fright and realize that all the stories are really nothing but stories. If you have passed over one or two periods after the first one made its appearance, it does not mean that you are going to become crazy, that something is wrong with you, but that the fright, the tales you have heard and the sensitive condition at your age have all affected your nervous system, and you will come out all right after you possess a full knowledge of these things as we go on from Chat to Chat.

The average American girl commences to menstruate at about fourteen years of age. Now if you have menstruated two years earlier or two years later it means nothing but a condition of your race, how you have lived, in the country or the excitements of the city, and other social conditions. From the time a girl first menstruates she can count on about thirty years of activity for the ovaries and womb. That is, if a girl menstruates for the first time at fourteen years of age, she ought not to have any cessation of the periods until she is forty-five years of age. So you can see that the later she is in starting, the later she will be in stopping. Of course the same thing happens when the girl commences to menstruate earlier, she will stop earlier.

The ovaries are two little sack-like organs lying on each side, in the pelvis, or the groin. From each ovary runs a little tube to the womb, which is situated beneath them right in the middle of the body. Now every month the ovaries send down the tubes a little egg which lands in the upper part of the womb, and when the womb is full of blood, which occurs every month in the healthy girl, this egg is carried away in the blood.

I do not intend to talk to you about the process of procreation or the physiology of conception; all these matters you may read about in the many good books which have been written upon those subjects. What I want to tell you are facts and things not to be found in books and which will, if you guide yourself by them, make you a strong and healthy woman throughout all your life.

From the time you first realize that you are no longer a little girl, but growing into a woman, you should commence to take the best of care of the ovaries and the monthly flow. These ovaries hang in the body by very tender and delicate ligaments. Never mind the names the doctors call these cords or other ligaments; we are always going to speak in the simplest language, so that you may get a clear understanding for the advice I shall give you. These ovaries are sensitive to all movements of the body and to your emotions. Anger, outbursts of indignation and wrong reading, all these produce an effect upon the ovaries, especially so when your period is in full activity.

You may be a romping, strong girl with well-developed muscles and bones and never had to be careful of what you did. But when the age approaches where you begin to feel strange, somewhat timid, and have new ideas and peculiar thoughts, when the old kind of rough exercise tires your back, it means that your ovaries and womb are receiving more than the usual amount of blood and are in no condition to be harshly knocked about. At this time there may be slight bleeding from the nose, for the first time a soreness of the breasts and nipples, a light feeling in the head and a disposition to easily get out of patience with your companions and things about you. When these many different feelings come you may know that the ovaries are getting ready to prove that you are a woman in the making.

Now remember that the monthly flow of blood does not come from the ovaries, but from the inside of the womb. The ovaries make the eggs and send these eggs down into the womb, as I have told you. When you are married these eggs are made alive by the husband's germ of life and remain in the womb, growing for nine months, when the little babe is old enough to be born and make you the happiest woman alive—that is if you are in good health. As long as you are a virtuous girl the womb cleanses itself every month. Of course this does not take place after you are married, for if so, you can readily see that the blood would carry away the egg. And it will do this even after you are married and have a little live egg in you, if you have not taken care of both womb and ovaries. This condition may become a regular habit, and then you end in being the most miserable woman on earth.

Because these things have not plainly been told the girls is the cause for so much injury being done to the womb and ovaries while growing. You have not been warned that you should cease all rough play, active sports, should not stand all day upon your feet nor dance late into the night. Some girls have been brought up to be over-active at this time just to prove that they will not acknowledge that there is any change or difference in them. Nature always punishes such an insult to her laws, and the teacher who places such ideas in the girl's mind is generally one whom Nature has already punished by denying her any of the sweet and powerful instincts of woman. Have nothing to do with these unfortunate and harmful creatures. You must assist Nature in her attempts to make you a complete woman; give in to her by keeping quiet, not fretting nor getting angry because you have to give up some dance or basketball game. If you do not give up many of these pleasures when you are a growing girl, you will have to give them up later on in life; give them up forever.

For the first two years from the commencement of your first monthly period you should be quiet, obtain plenty of sleep and good food and take no exercise except walking, swimming and bending of the body in your room night and morning. Skating is not injurious if it is not overdone and you keep your feet dry and warm. Some girls have been injured for life—though they did not know it at the time—by sliding downhill on sleds. They were tossed off or ran into some post or fence and were slightly bruised. Such a slight accident caused a rupture or strain on the ovaries or womb, perhaps the tender ligaments were stretched and the ignorant girl continued her play with them in this condition.

Much of this advice may seem old-fashioned to you, but in all truth it is advice founded upon the NEW experience and knowledge of all physicians who have seen the havoc wrought by carelessness and ignorance in these matters.

The womb, hanging by its delicate cords, is at this time in the girl's life growing rapidly and consequently receiving plenty of new blood. It has not reached full development and it takes but little to put it out of place and have it stay there. The ovaries may be so twisted and put out of order that nothing can be done for them in later life but to cut them out with a knife; then you are ruined as far as womanhood is concerned.

Young age has wonderful powers of repairing injuries. If it were not so, but few would ever reach full growth. But there are some injuries youth cannot correct, and these are the distortions and displacements of woman's sex organs—the internal ones. If you jar or tear these organs, the ovaries and womb, while you are growing, you do not know of the injury at the time. Everything at this age is strange to you in feeling and function, and slight pains in the back or groin, irregularity or too little flow, you think is nothing. But it is EVERYTHING to you when you reach the marriageable age, or when your time comes to become a mother.

The womb is pear-shaped, big end upwards. It should hang nearly straight in the body. The small end is the outlet which opens at the time the baby is to be born. It also opens slightly every month to let out the blood, then closes when it has emptied itself. Now you can readily see that if it is twisted, tipped backwards or otherwise out of shape, birth can only be given at great risk to both the babe and its mother. It may be out of place so that nothing but an operation will save life. It may be so turned backward that the child is smothered while trying to grow, and then must come a horrible operation. Even the unmarried woman will suffer from any of these misplacements of the womb. Every month the blood tries to pass off it finds obstruction; pains, griping pains occur, sometimes the blood cannot pass away but remains to cause inflammations and tumors, and unless corrected by an operation the poor woman's life is one of torture and invalidism.

Ignorant, never having been told of these important matters, you may have tried to vault in the gymnasiums, played a fierce game of basketball or gone to a dance when your flow was on. This, strange as it may seem to some, is the most frequent cause of "Women's Troubles," "Female Weakness," etc. Now there is absolutely no reason for a woman to have "troubles" or "weakness." Nature has so made woman that in reality she can stand much more strain and endurance of a certain kind than man can. At the start she is possessed of everything which makes a strong and well being throughout all her life. She has to be of this nature, for just think, she does the work of two beings. While the child is growing in the womb she has to watch and feed herself to give the little one good blood—HER blood. When it is born, she has to do the same thing—give it good, health-giving milk. Then as the child leaves her breasts, she has to watch and care for all its growing years. Besides all these cares she has her household, her husband, her hundred and one duties to perform. Surely all this requires a strength of body, a determined will and an all-absorbing love. No man could or would do all this—Never!

A perfectly well woman, a woman whose sexual parts are in their places and strongly attached there, does all this tremendous work happy, smiling, and reaches the grandmother's chair with the sweetest countenance to be seen on a human face.

It used to be so; we see but few happy and uncomplaining mothers now. And there is but one cause for all the present misery and race suicide.

Ignorance of sex laws and prudery in all the most vital matters pertaining to young girls is the reason and cause.

No exercise which puts a strain on the body should ever be taken by the growing girl. Especially true is this when you are having your menstrual period, for then you should be as quiet as possible. In many cases it would be best for the girl to remain away from school. If you have to go to school, that is if you cannot make your mother understand the matter, you should be allowed to sit and not stand at your lessons. Every girl should be placed in the unembarrassing position to leave and go home at any time during school hours.

Thousands of girls have been ruined in health because their male teacher or gymnasium instructor could see only a pupil and not a growing woman, because a condition which should excuse one girl or make allowance for another, or a state of sexual nervousness which means the girl ought to be sent home at once, are subjects that are not talked over between a male principal and a woman teacher—that is, not as they should be talked over. It is an old story to the doctor, these nervous and sexually-ill young women. Taken unwell in school, perhaps suffering pains caused by a previous "standing it out," the poor girl increases the injury to her organs, and besides being unable to put her mind upon her school work, she suffers the humiliation of a low mark.

But we cannot do these necessary things at the public schools, girls so often tell me. Well, there is but one answer to such a complaint. If the schools are so regulated that a growing girl cannot have the best of care, consideration and instruction in these vital matters, we had better close them all—every one. But what we can do is to have schools for girls only, and these must have teachers whose first thoughts are the physical welfare of all the pupils and who are thoroughly conversant with sex hygiene and all this means to the future women of our land.

I have to speak of this most important matter to you girls because in a few years most of you will have daughters to send to school, and as it is almost a hopeless task to bring the present generation out of their mucilaginous prudery, YOU must take hold as mothers and demand that such care and instruction will be given your girls that we shall no longer have this sad condition of suffering and childless women as has existed the last forty years or so. You will find the young men of your generation aiding and forcing these common-sense forms of education, for they, too, are being instructed in the matter from their side of the question.

I remember a beautiful girl of fifteen years of age, who was brought to me suffering from a nervous breakdown. There was nothing the matter with her except everything. Never having had that care and instruction she should have had, one day in school her pains became unbearable. She cried, and when she went to ask her teacher to excuse her, this misfit of a teacher sent the embarrassed girl to the PRINCIPAL. Of course she would not go and tell HIM what the trouble was; she left of her own accord and was marked for it. But this was not the worst of it; some evil-minded boys in her class laughed at her when she returned a few days afterwards and uttered those despicable hints which go straight to a good girl's heart. And she never told her mother, because her mother had never told her anything. A girl in the school—oh, there are a lot of these kinds, I dare say you all know one or two of them—told her what to do to keep the monthly flow away.

So she finally had to go to the doctor, who found a frightful state of things—one ovary ruined for life. For three years she remained an invalid, and the shock she received, added to the drugs she had taken, had made her one of those many unfortunate women which fill our land.

All heavy lifting is dangerous to the womb and ovaries during the growing period; therefore all the apparatus in the gymnasiums for testing the strength of arms and back should be avoided. Many a foolish or uninstructed girl has made herself a girl of muscles, but ruined her WOMANLY POWERS in so doing. Save all your strength and force for what Nature intended a woman to DO; don't throw it away in doing gymnasium stunts. No real youth or man likes to see a girl do these things; his applause does not come from the heart, but only from the head. Such a girl may have strong arms in which to carry a baby, but the chances are some other woman will have to give her the baby to carry. Of course every girl should exercise, but it must be such exercises as is governed with her sexual organs ever in view. As an example, dancing is good recreation and exercise, but it should not be indulged in two days BEFORE the menstrual period and not until two days AFTER.

Another thing which affects the womb—retention of urine. That is, keeping the bladder full. Many girls have been brought up in such ignorance and under such false ideas of prudery that they will suffer pain from distention of the bladder rather than allow the slightest hint to escape them that they need immediate relief. This brings about not only a weakness of the bladder, which will in later life be very annoying and really embarrassing, but the pressure of a full bladder on the surrounding parts—the womb and its attachments—is apt to displace it and irritate it. Then again, a girl may be within a few days of her flow, and here the pressure of a full and hard bladder may set up an inflammation and bring on the period before its time. All this tends to start an irregularity, and when this irregularity is fairly established, the girl's, and later on the woman's, life is only an existence full of misery.

In fact, I think I am justified in saying that ninety per cent. of the women suffering from nervousness, hysteria, restlessness and pain, comes from the sexual organs being out of place, twisted, early inflammations and general lack of care of them from want of knowledge.

And it is so easy for a girl to grow into complete womanhood, full of life, good health and scarcely any unnatural knowledge that she has ovaries, womb or breasts. Most women to-day only know they have a womb from the severe pains and that "bearing down" feeling about which they constantly complain.

Please understand that in this CHAT we are only considering general and common conditions which injure all growing girls and result in miserable health in after life. I am only hinting about the errors due to ignorance which produce our hysterical women and childless wives. And I want to repeat this fact, that there is absolutely no reason for all this invalidism and suffering among women and girls.

The general rules I shall give you for perfect condition and good health must be followed by all girls and young women, but I shall have to devote some time to the special needs of girls who work in shops, large stores, factories and those who are brought into close intimacy with men in offices.

Those dragging pains in the small of the back so many suffer from during the menstrual flow, and those racking headaches, are not natural. The pains mean that the womb is dragging or else pulling upon its supports;

that you need to rest and keep off your feet as much as possible. If you are a schoolgirl, you MUST stay at home and rest upon your back much of the time. There is no excuse for your not doing this. To force you to go to school to take an examination or make up a certain lesson is criminal. STRIKE! It would be a good thing if you all formed a union for the protection of your future health, and demanded your sex rights. Rest you should, and must, from all mental or physical excitement if you wish to be a woman who will be a blessing to those around her instead of a burden.

Which had you rather YOUR daughter should have, a certificate of perfect health, with the knowledge that when she marries she can become a mother without danger to herself and child, that she can remain happy in the nursery instead of miserable in the hospital, or a diploma stating that she can read French poetry and write an essay upon "Woman's Career"?

Some of these statements you girls will have to read to your mothers. Then if prudery has blinded them to the truth, take the matter into your own hands. It is upon you, in the future, that depends the decent regulating of instruction in the public schools. The girl who goes to dances or any evening entertainment lightly clothed, low neck and short sleeves, while she is menstruating, as thousands do, will certainly land in the doctor's hands or become one of those pitiful things, a drug fiend. And the drug habit starts from taking "some harmless thing" to ease the pains or stop the flow.

That curse of the American girls, constipation, does as much if not more, to hurt the womb than a full bladder. We shall have a lot to say about this matter later on in our Chats about the skin and complexion.

When the menstrual period first makes its appearance the swelling and tenderness of the breasts, the itching, a feeling of fullness in the region of the womb, are all natural and should not cause any worry. If you are in perfect health and KEEP so, these little symptoms will become less noticeable as you grow into full womanhood. So do not get frightened, do not take any medicines nor act upon the foolish advice from other girls. The flashes of heat, frequent blushing, dizziness and the frequent desire to pass your water, are all natural. There are some fortunate girls who approach and pass this first period without all these uncomfortable symptoms, but most of you will have some or all of them.

The itching of the skin, pimples on the face and body, sometimes a sore throat, all these are nothing but indications of the great revolution you are going through from being a girl to becoming a glorious woman. Then there are the toilet duties to be done at this period and throughout your life which make for perfect health.

Oh, yes, I shall tell you all about these matters and what to do.

During the periods of the first year or so you are in a condition to catch many of the diseases all around you, such as tuberculosis—consumption—erysipelas, tonsilitis, scarlet fever and the mumps. Remember I do not say you are liable to catch such a disease as consumption, only that you are in a condition when the germs can find lodgment better than at other times. Of course you should never sleep in a room with a consumptive or even be around one at any time, but should it happen that during your developing period anyone with the disease was liable to be brought into contact with you, keep away, away in the open air.

At this period also mumps may be a serious matter for you, so if you have a little brother or sister who is suffering from this disease of childhood, you should keep out of the room and, if possible, out of the house. No matter if you did have the mumps when a little girl. If you catch the mumps during the first years of your young womanhood the affection MAY go to your ovaries. This, of course, produces a painful swelling and, if not attended to by a reputable physician, will go to destroy the usefulness of the ovaries—prevent you from ever having children. This has happened in girls who did not know—or rather their mothers did not know—what the danger was, and when the girl grew up to be married and no children came, she was blamed, often accused of being one who did not want children. Many a time when a young woman had been married several years and was childless, I have asked the mother if her daughter had the mumps when she was growing into womanhood, and if she suffered pain in the groin and back.

"Why, yes, Doctor—but what has that to do with it?"

"Didn't you know that the mumps sometimes went to the ovaries and destroyed their function?"

"Why, no; it can't be possible?"

"Yes, possible and probable. Your daughter can never have children because you did not tell her all about her sex organs, and when her little brother had a swelling and pain in the glands of throat and jaws, you did not know enough to send her away or keep her away from him, telling her plainly why you did so.

"But you were never allowed to mention these things when you were a young woman—you never knew these important things? Exactly so, and this is the punishment thousands of mothers and daughters are receiving for this prudery."

Chapter III

The Disorders of Menstruation and General Health

Civilization has brought many unnatural effects upon the monthly period of women, and ignorance of how to care for the body has made matters worse. It is with these unnatural disturbances that you are mostly concerned. The inability to understand certain symptoms of your menstrual flow, the consequent neglect of these symptoms or ignorantly taking drugs and medicines for the troubles, are the causes for so many girls and women being miserable and invalids struggling on under most distressing conditions.

There is always a good cause for any irregularity or stoppage of the monthly period; some reason why the flow is scanty or too profuse. These causes can readily be discovered when the girl knows herself and all that pertains to that self.

In the healthy girl the flow should come and go without any marked pains or distress. Of course during four or five days there will be a feeling of weakness, lassitude, a "please-let-me-alone" attitude, and in many girls, a desire for pure love and caresses. These various feelings are natural and only go to show that you are a full-blown woman.

There is nothing to be ashamed of in this feeling for love and caresses, this peculiar desire to want protection and a something that you cannot exactly explain to yourself. It is really an awakening of all your womanly desires, and these are your greatest powers over man, children and the best of everything in the world. These feelings should not be suppressed, but kept under control. They should be carefully saved, for they are the feelings which bring future happiness, and you want to give them as little attention as possible except that attention which keeps them pure and holy.

Avoid all women who scoff at motherhood, who deride the domestic life for women, who stand and shout their demands in public places instead of sweetly using their influence for a better condition for men and women so that the future babies will have a proper birthright. No discussion or knowledge which will make better fathers and mothers can be wrong, but every attempt to ignore the subject is sinful.

There is nothing to be ashamed of in maternal feeling and impulses; what a girl is to be blamed for is a want of control over these natural instincts and giving way to them. The care of the company she keeps, the kind of thoughts she lets get into her mind and the way she cares for her body, are the factors which make for a good and chaste girl or otherwise.

But how can we blame all those girls who accidentally go wrong? I certainly do not. They have never been told just what to do, where the danger lurks and all the consequences. Should we blame and shun the girls who have been sent out into the world amid the dangers and snares laid for them; young women who see chastity mocked, virtue a thing to bargain for, the glitter of gold pouring into the laps of those thousands who find "the easiest way" out of their poverty and struggles?

Yet the truth is, hard as it may seem and as often as it has been told to you, that virtue and chastity in deeds and thoughts DO bring rich awards. These awards may be a long and tedious time in coming and the struggle is hard, but in the end all this will be proven to have been worth while.

As I have told you, the monthly period should come and go without much physical pain. It should last from four to five days and be regular in recurring about every twenty-eight days. But it is seldom so normal in the average American girl, the girl who has been left alone to solve her own mysteries and go her own way. This is equally true of the high-school girl or the working girl. And why? Because she has been brought up through her early developing days to go on and disregard all her sex functions—the greatest factor in all life. The high-school girl has been mixed up with all kinds of youths and not kept away from tantalizing and embarrassing conditions. The shop and working-girl has been forced to do her work, day in and out, standing upon her feet or working at a machine while the sensitive and full-blooded womb was trying to empty itself.

Let us first consider the girl whose monthly flow is scanty or entirely absent. She has arrived at the age of sixteen years and has not "seen anything." But every month, for a year or so, she has had headaches, felt extremely nervous, had some pains, the breasts have felt tender and sore, and altogether she has had a miserable twelve months of these symptoms, but no relief from a flow. What is the matter with such a girl?

Remember I told you that the womb was pear-shaped, the small end hanging down. Here is a little opening, through which the menstrual blood flows, and then out of the body. The womb is in reality only a big bunch of muscles so arranged that it can relax and empty itself and then tightly close. In the unmarried woman, or before one has given birth to a child, this little opening is completely closed except during the period. Even then it is only very slightly opened, but open and shut it must if a girl is to be in good health.

A girl may have over-exercised or injured herself when she was twelve years of age or thereabouts, and brought about a little inflammation, which at the time she knew nothing about. The womb was already getting prepared to do its monthly work, and as the weeks went on the inflammation increased. Inflammation always means some kind of an extra growth at the injured spot; like a scar, for example, after a wound has healed up.

The womb itself is not a sensitive organ to the touch or to slight inflammations at the lower end, hence the little girl does not, at the time, feel any pain. She may feel uncomfortable in that region, but as she has been brought up NEVER to mention any matters concerning her sex organs, of course she keeps silent while the injury goes on. The little inflammation heals up, but in healing what does it do? Leaves a scar, of course. Now this scar may be big enough to have CLOSED the outlet for the monthly flow—to have made the entrance of the womb grow together. It is under these circumstances a sealed bag; nothing can come away from it.

The girl's time comes, but the blood does not. All the other signs being present, she watches and worries. Sometimes, alas, too many times, she has never been told just what should happen. Backache troubles her, headaches often drives her to take some harmful drug, she becomes fretful, loses control of her temper in the simplest things and finally loses friends because she "is so horrid, says so many cutting things."

Yet she does not mean to be disagreeable; she simply cannot help it. How could she? There is a clot of blood in her womb that cannot come away; it remains and hardens and each month is added to by the banked-up blood.

It is a very sad condition, and one that often continues until a tumor is formed, or some other complication makes an invalid of her in the prime of her life—or what should be her prime.

This condition is frequently the cause of hysteria, of desperation, of a gradual mental failing.

There is another condition which goes to ruin a girl's health and happiness, for the effects are the same as in a closed womb. There is a membrane in all chaste girls called the hymen. This closes the entrance to the vagina. Now there should always be a little opening, or several little openings in this membrane to let out the blood. In some girls this is closed from birth; so completely closed and tough that the weight of the first monthly blood cannot break through it. Then we have all the symptoms of the stoppage we have in the closed womb, only the blood packs and hardens in the lower parts instead of the womb. Often this produces greater distress than when the same conditions exist in the womb. Here great bloody tumors form and the state of the poor girl is certainly pitiable.

From birth also the womb may be closed, grown together. Then there are some girls so nervously constituted that the least touch on the muscles of the womb will shut it up spasmodically. Such a girl's womb is not grown together, but when the first drops of blood are trying to ooze away, the womb shuts tightly. In all these cases the results to the girl is the same as I have described.

The remedy for all this misery is simple, almost painless, and will not detain you from your duties but a few days; sometimes not at all. By simply cutting or snipping apart the growth at the entrance to the organ, or opening it by a little stretching instrument, the fault is remedied; the girl cured. And all this simple knowledge could have saved thousands of suffering girls and women. No, it does not interfere with your proof of virginity. The snipping is too slight. But supposing it should? What of it, as long as you know in your own heart that your are a chaste girl? Do you want to be a miserable wreck of a woman just on account of an ancient superstition, a foolish and harmful idea of a lot of old women and medieval theologians?

It is a sad condition—this closed womb—and should not be allowed to sicken a girl for one hour—IF SHE KNOWS.

Alas! she has not been allowed to know these things—just allowed to suffer and be blamed.

If you have reached the age of fifteen years or thereabouts and for a year or so have had all the nervous and mental symptoms of a period occurring every month and no blood comes, then go at once to a reputable physician. Be certain you go to one in good standing. Never go to one who advertises "women's troubles," or to one whom you do not know by the best of repute. Remember that honest and true physicians do not advertise in the papers. So whenever you see an advertisement of a doctor who says he can cure you of THAT trouble, keep away from him. Never mind what the other girls tell you about a doctor or some medicine that cured them, probably the cause for their trouble was an entirely different one.

Naturally, your mother is the first one to consult, but I fear that if you have a mother who has allowed you to suffer month after month, and constantly said, “Oh, don’t bother about such matters; it will come out all right when you get older;” such a mother will not exactly be the one to go to—go to a RELIABLE physician.

Never, under any circumstances, take medicines for this trouble. Let “regulating pills” alone as you would a rattlesnake. Now that you know the cause, common-sense will tell you that pills, or any and all things of the kind, are not only useless, but harmful.

“But, Doctor, how about the girl who has had several good periods and then stops for several months, or even skips a month and only flows every other month? There can be no closing of the mouth of the womb under these circumstances?”

No, in such cases the cause is entirely different, or rather the causes, for there are many. Most of you can find out for yourself just what YOUR cause is for being irregular, after I point out to you some facts.

Many times it is only Nature’s way of preserving your health. For instance, if you have not sufficient blood in your system to allow you to lose a certain amount every month, Nature will prevent it going to the womb to be thrown away. Some girls will have “nose bleeds” once or twice a month and this takes the place of the monthly flow. This is not a sign of good health, just a sign that something is wrong—see a good doctor, he will know and tell you what to do. If you are troubled with headaches (especially in the back of the head and neck), if your appetite is poor, if you lost too great an amount during your last flow, or if your nervousness increases, it means that you are in poor condition. Perhaps you have danced too much and lost too much sleep, been unduly excited or had some great grief; any of these things will affect in some way your menses. Anything, in fact, which lowers the tone of your general health will affect the menses.

If you are over-fat and growing fatter every day, this unhealthful condition will stop your menses. I don’t mean a plump, jolly, happy amount of fat,—this is a good state for a growing girl,—but I mean an overplus of fat with white cheeks, flabby flesh, swollen ankles and big stomach. Such a condition indicates some disease.

There are many diseases which leave you in a condition of suppressed or irregular menstruation; such as typhoid fever, kidney affections, chlorosis—lack of red blood—consumption, scarlet fever. If you have gone through any one of these illnesses and your periods are irregular or scanty, don't worry; time will put this matter right as you recover from the general effects of the disease. If you have reason to fear consumption, be grateful that Nature is preserving your blood to help you get well; for, as you know, you can get well—can completely recover from consumption—if you WILL EAT AND SLEEP IN THE OPEN AIR—LIVE IN THE OPEN AIR.

Most of the causes for irregularities and scanty flows are due to your unhygienic methods of living and playing. Sleeping in rooms where fresh air only gets in through a crack, insufficient and improper food and too much tea and coffee, will soon cause irregularities and other menstrual troubles. Catching cold or getting wet feet, damp skirts flapping around thinly-clad ankles just before or during the time of your monthlies, will also bring you to some womb trouble.

Then the influence of the mind upon all these matters plays a very important part in your health. Evil suggestions from girls or youths, seeing plays which you ought not to see, reading all that rotten stuff put out for young women and girls to read and dream over—I don't mean the nasty ones, but all those which unduly excite the imagination and throw a false light upon life—the Duke, the Prince and Villain kind—the virtuous blonde maiden and the hard-working hero stuff, you all know what I mean. There is plenty of good literature, exciting stories, to be read without reading a lot of cheap tinsel and ready-made romances which have no more to do with real life than a mask has to do with the human features.

You can over-exercise, become too much excited over contests in the gymnasium, use up force to such an extent that your growing womanly functions become weakened and sometimes dried up. No girl of a nervous temperament should go into any athletic contest, team or personal. Such a girl should not play basketball, attempt any stunts on horizontal bars or flying rings; nothing, in fact, which calls for a strain upon the nervous system. The function of the womb, as well as of all the sex organs, are directly affected by the nervous system. You can never be a strong woman, complete in all that belongs to a woman and her career, if you, as a young woman, over-strain the nervous system.

Hundreds of girls who are playing contests of basketball, to see which team is to be the champion of the state or the town, are going to suffer from all this excitement. Your teachers do not take into serious consideration your growing sex organs. They do not seem to know what it means for a girl to get over-excited at any time during her development, that there is nothing except alcohol which will arouse dangerous impulses more than athletic excitement. So do be careful of your exercise.

On the other hand, no exercise will also produce some disturbance of the menstrual period. If you do not take some form of useful exercise, poisons accumulate in your system. This causes unnatural fat to pile up around your ovaries and kidneys; in fact, it will bring you to a sad state in middle life if you have neglected to exercise in a careful and regular manner when you are growing.

The girl who works in the shop, the department store, or follows any of the numerous careers which are open to her, as a rule gets plenty of exercise. To be sure it is not the best kind of exercise by any means, but as she has to be on her feet almost all the day, for her to take any gymnasium work at night is harmful. She needs the fresh air, to eat proper food and to obtain plenty of sleep—all she can get or steal. The girl who is so situated that she can walk to and from her place of employment, is fortunate; the girl who cannot, must get walking exercise in the open air some way if she wishes her periods and general health to be perfect.

Profuse menstruation, that is, too much blood flowing and for too long a time, is always a sign that something is wrong with the womb as well as with your general health. It is not a sign that "you have too much blood in your system," but a symptom that the womb is weak, has lost its tone and does not close up tightly at the finish as it should. The cause is one of the many I have told you about; too long standing on the feet, going to parties or dances when you should have been in bed, improper food or too little of it, undue excitement at a time when you should have been quiet. Search well your own heart, and some of the causes you will be able to discover yourself. In other words, any irregularity or little errors in your conduct will bring about irregularity in your menstrual functions.

No girl should use the sewing machine when she is unwell, or do any work which involves the movement of the thighs and legs.

Food, nourishment and clothing have a lot to do with all the irregularities and disturbances of the sex organs, but we shall have to chat about these important matters when dealing with the skin and complexion, so leave them here. It will save repeating.

One great curse—for that is what it really is—of all American girls and women, is constipation. False modesty, ignorance and not drinking enough water are the principal causes for this injurious state. But never mind the causes, let us get at the effects.

Every portion of your body, including the bones, can be in a state of good health only when constantly supplied with fresh water. Coffee, soda water, chocolate or other makeshifts do not take the place of pure water. You should get the water into you daily, by the quart. I wish I could go into this matter so thoroughly as to make you all see and understand the importance of this fact. However, I can show you in these Chats how necessary it is even to your sex organs and what they throw off, to make you, I hope, drink plenty of water throughout all your lives.

The bowels must be emptied every day. Any keeping of the cast-off material of the intestines in the bowels means an odorous skin, foul breath and other disagreeable odors, no matter how clean you may be OUTWARDLY. Then there is another very important feature of this dried-up state. As you grow older the arteries harden, they cannot expand and contract as the blood pressure demands they should, and when any strain comes upon the heart or blood vessels, these latter burst and apoplexy is the result.

But before this takes place there has been a failing of the memory, perhaps of the intellect, because the proper amount of blood needed to nourish the brain cannot pass through the tiny, but important arteries of the brain. So some kind of softening of the brain follows. "She died from apoplexy" is said. No, she died because, when a young woman, she would not drink water in sufficient quantities to keep her organs flushed and clear of accumulated material. Now, if this absence of water in the system so affects the brain, its arteries and veins, just imagine what trouble the womb will have in getting enough water for all its needed blood.

But there is a more important effect that the absence of plenty of water in the system has upon the girl. It is a very serious matter to her, as it affects her attractiveness and happiness, and this is what we want to get at in these Chats.

You all know that at certain times girls will have more or less an odor from their skins and breaths. It is very noticeable in some girls, and in others of the most careful cleanliness and habits it will be detected. Perfumery only makes matters worse; the attempt to cover the natural odors is too marked.

These odors are all caused by acids and other chemical materials which exist in the natural secretions of the body; the perspiration, breath and other secretions. The less water there is in the human system, the more will these chemical odors pervade the atmosphere surrounding the girl.

It is the lack of plenty of water that causes the skin to give forth odors. If you have exercised to the extent of bringing on profuse perspiration and have not drank plenty of water before, during and after the exercise, no amount of bathing will prevent an odor coming from the skin. If you are going out to a dance or any place where you will be in a warm room, you will not be able to disguise the chemical odors coming from the skin.

But if you have filled your system with water two or three hours before going out, your skin will have a delicious, natural odor.

During the menstrual period every gland in the growing girl is very active. The skin throws off an extra amount of perspiration, the glands under the arms are very, extremely, active. Then at this time the breath comes faster than usual and throws off its poisons in large quantities. All these off-castings of the body are loaded with material that must leave the body if we are to keep in good health. But here is the point. You can so saturate your system with pure water that all these fatty and acid odors become highly diluted and scarcely any of them will make their presence known to those around you.

Drinking water will make you fat? Nonsense. That is some old woman's tale—some old woman who tries to excuse herself from drinking water. Water will not make you fat nor make you lean; just keep you in the good health and state you were born to be in. Then it helps keep the bowels clean, gives a good flow to the blood and keeps the womb free from any little clots being left over from your last menstruation.

How much water shall I drink? Two tumblerfuls every morning before breakfast, two between each meal and as much at meals as you want. Don't bother yourself about the fads of drinking water, such as none at meals, for instance.

Look at a horse; he drinks when he is thirsty and he drinks all he wants. Take water away from a horse, keep it away from him as it has been kept away from girls and young women, and you would soon see his coat become dull, sticky, and the light go from his eyes.

Remember that a horse's coat of hair corresponds to your skin; it is his complexion. Deprive yourself of water and your skin becomes dull, sticky and malodorous. But we shall have a lot to say about the skin, so nothing more now.

With all this good habit of drinking plenty of water must go the application of water to the outside of the body. This you must do to wash away the dried crystals of all the chemical materials sent out from the skin and glands. Warm SPONGE baths, while you are menstruating, are necessary. I know that you all have been told never to take a bath while your period was on, but you see that you must get rid of these tell-tale odors now that you are out in the world. Of course you must be careful not to take cold; you should not use any but warm water, and then jump into bed warmly covered. Use no scented soap, not even under the arms, just plain castile or a similar PURE soap. After the flow has ceased be certain to wash your external parts with a soft sponge and pure soap. You want to consider this part of your toilet just as important as washing the teeth or ears, and it should be done in the same unconcerned and unthinking manner.

Chapter IV

The Care of the Skin and Complexion

All girls want a good complexion and a clear skin. The skin and hair are the glories of a healthy woman. Most of you can have this desired state of a clear skin and pure complexion. A good complexion merely means a perfect state of health. A clear skin does not depend on what you apply to it, but what you keep off it.

The clear, satin-like skin, the skin which looks like a transparent piece of silk laid upon a soft cushion of white flesh, and that sheeny skin resembling fine velvet, seen in the pure blonde type of girls, are all the effects of the blood beneath and how that blood is treated by the emotions.

Muddy and contaminating thoughts will cause a muddy skin. Clean and clear thoughts will give you a clear skin. Jealousy and anger will, in time, affect the flow of blood through your tiny skin-veins and give you the appearance of age. Any emotion which causes indigestion will do the same thing. In fact, the state of mind and the manner in which you control your thoughts and temper are reflected in the tone of the skin.

It is during the first few years of menstruating that the girl who does not understand these matters commences to ruin her complexion. While your body is developing, the tiny glands in the skin are undergoing great changes. These changes cause the glands to pour out oily matter, perspiration and other material, all of which naturally bring about a muddy complexion in some girls and redness of the nose, or pimples on the face, in others.

These conditions are natural to the growing girl. The skin is clearing itself of all the little girl's activities and making ready for the woman's complexion. It is Springtime with the skin, and this dirt—or what looks like dirt—is the result of all this skin-cleaning. Hair is appearing on certain parts of the body; that almost invisible down which all women possess, is growing on all portions of the body and face. The monthly periods are causing congested blood vessels throughout the whole body and especially the tiny arteries of the skin. Every part of your system is really undergoing a great change and does not get into a state of perfect health until you are eighteen years of age and over. As in all things in which a decided revolution takes place, there is more or less of a disturbance.

This is the time when a girl commences to worry about her complexion. She frets and becomes anxious about the little spots appearing upon her face. If she has not the proper home advice, but hears all sorts of tales and sees all sorts of things in the school or shop, she soon resorts to the drug stores for a face lotion, powder or cream. She may have been told by an older girl that, "No, I never had anything but a good complexion; you'd better take something for yours, I would," and much more of this kind of foolish advice.

Some girls go through the period of development without any marked change in their complexion; others, especially brunettes, will have a "broken-out-face," a hot and oily skin and not infrequently pimples on some part of their bodies. Girls of nervous temperament are apt to have more or less of a spotted complexion during the first few years of menstruation. In all these girls it is more of a sign of good health than otherwise, and if the skin had been left alone,—which it has not, because you have never known the truth,—the quack advertisements of "face creams," "skin food," "complexion wafers," and all the other skin poisons and complexion-destroyers, would never have been put out to swindle girls and women.

Pimples most frequently show on the shoulders and upper arms, and unless the girl knows that these really mean a splendid complexion when she has grown to full womanhood, she worries herself to a point that makes her little life miserable.

This is the point in a girl's life where she starts in to ruin her complexion forever. She commences to fill in the openings made to let out the fatty and other substances in her skin, by powdering, applying some ointment which keeps these pores closed, or goes to bed with greasy or other injurious "skin foods" upon her face. In fact, she does just what in the end will give her a pasty complexion instead of a clear one. Of course she will later on take to the rouge and powder puffs and have to keep them in constant use until her skin becomes like that of a dried codfish.

Please remember that what you need during the first years of your menstrual life is to allow full freedom for the skin to get rid of all the material your state is producing behind the outer skin. This material must come away if the skin is to be a clear and healthy one. Banking up, stopping this sweating process of the glands of the body, will ruin your complexion in time. You would not attempt to clean a room by sweeping all the dust under the carpet and not expect this dust to be always flying up and making the room dusty and ill-smelling? But you do about the same thing when you do not let all the dirt and dust come away through the spring cleaning of the skin.

The period of your development is the Springtime of your life, and you must expect all kinds of disagreeable feelings and little annoyances to occur during this period.

Each month, just as your menses are coming on, you will find little pimples or some redness on your face, nose or shoulders; perhaps on the arms. You should not want to go to dances or entertainments at these times; in fact you should not; but at no time during your growth into full womanhood should you wear gowns with short sleeves and low necks. For even between the menstrual periods there will be some indications upon the face or skin which tell the story. To hide these little eruptions or redness of the skin you have to apply powder to the neck, shoulders and arms. What are the consequences? The perspiration, due to the heat of the room and the exercise of dancing, keeps the inflammation active under the powder and may cause such pimples that the scars are left forever.

And right here is where you "catch cold." Drafts, sleeping by an open window or going from a warm room to a colder one do not give you a cold. You may catch cold by doing these things, but the cause is something which has brought about a too rapid loss of heat from the body; such as any wrong way of clothing or underclothing yourself; low-neck dresses for winter; or covering the skin with powder or enamel, through which the perspiration cannot have free play and keep the temperature of the body equal; these are the reasons you "catch cold."

Those girls you occasionally see with a pitted skin on their faces and shoulders, are those who in all probability prevented the natural grease and other substances from getting out when they were in the first two or three years of their development. They have generally brought about this disagreeable complexion by attempting to dress as full-grown women and covering face, shoulders and backs with some kind of lotion, powder or cream.

The girl who was noted for her fine, soft and smooth skin when she was eight or ten years of age, commences at puberty to have pimples and blackheads on her nose, cheeks and forehead. This being about the time she takes more notice of herself and others around her, these little facial blotches worry her. It is the opening of a new life and much attention is given dress, hair and complexion; to her whole appearance. She brushes and fixes her hair with great care; tries all sorts of experiments. She probably uses the brush of her older sister or one belonging to some of her family, or more frequently it is the common one at school or in the store. She does not intentionally use a dirty brush, nor will she use one which she has the least suspicion has been used by the unclean. But even the brush of her mother or sister carries germs that at this time do much injury to her skin and scalp, because the skin of the forehead is affected by the germs which get to the scalp.

This germ is one which is always to be found in the glands of any person's scalp or hairy portions of the body. These glands are known as the sebaceous glands. They are the ones which secrete the oily substance that is necessary for the health of the skin and hair. You have enough of the oily substances in your own hair and skin, and it is usually free from germs at this time if you have used only YOUR OWN BRUSH. But the moment you use a brush belonging to some older and full-grown woman you carry to your own scalp these germs. If some of the other germs which are sometimes found upon common brushes get onto your scalp, there is another trouble for you to combat—dandruff. In the first case you simply add oily stuff to your own supply, get over-much of the oil; in the other case, dandruff is piled thick with the fatty material and then comes scalp disease.

This may go on for some time and not noticeably affect you, but it may cause in a few weeks a certain form of eczema about the forehead and even the face. This is a very important matter for all girls and young women to remember. I have shown you that on the approach and for some time after puberty, all the tiny glands of the skin are enlarged and very active, so you can now see that there are hundreds of thousands of little holes for the germs to get into, and they do so from the brushes you are in the habit of using—that is, most of you. When these germs have located themselves upon the scalp, they soon commence to show the fact by giving you a muddy complexion. Sometimes you will be accused of not thoroughly washing your face, so marked is the line around your forehead and neck made by the attack of these germs. When the openings of the glands begin to gape, the effect is not agreeable to you nor to your friends.

The pimples commence to irritate you on account of the increase of the oily substance, and soon you see that little creamy spot, then you or a misguided friend will squeeze it out. Often before this harmful procedure is gone through with, a formation of a little cocoon-like body is formed and then you have blackheads. This is not all dirt as is generally supposed, but a little cylinder filled with fatty stuff, water and some dirt from the skin. If these blackheads keep coming and if you go on squeezing them, if you insist upon covering the pimples with powder or lotion, a real skin disease will be the result. This skin disease we call acne, and it is a difficult and trying one to cure. Never mind all those fetching advertisements in the papers which claim to cure acne in a few applications. Don't touch such harmful stuff. All these advertised lotions simply COVER UP the symptoms of the disease, drive it further into the skin, and when you finally have to go to a reputable doctor, too much harm has been done for him to save you from being marked for life. Never trifle with advertised cures, go to a well-known doctor, or if you cannot afford to pay a specialist's price, seek one at the outdoor clinics. There you will receive the same kind and careful treatment you would if you went to his office in an automobile of your own.

What are we to do to keep from having all these disagreeable pimples and their after-effects? Prevent them. You understand; not cure, but prevention; for I want to put you all in a position to keep from having any trouble which needs a CURE in the medical sense.

The first thing to do is to look out for your scalp as soon as you recognize the approach of puberty and for ever after. I do not mean that even a little girl should ever have her scalp neglected, but that you must, as soon as your menstrual time comes, NEVER use any other brush than your own and this must be a new one. No matter how old you are, get a new brush every few months and guard it as you would your jewels or your most precious gift. You should consider a brush for the hair as sacred as the one for your teeth. You surely would not think of brushing your teeth with any old toothbrush which happened to come along; neither should you use any other hairbrush but your own.

And all this is such a simple matter, for whatever you do, wherever you go, whether you attend school, work in an office or store, you can easily carry with you your own hairbrush as you do your own toothbrush. Of course the same rule applies to comb, soap and towel.

The habit some girls have of brushing and combing each other's hair is all very well if only your brush is used upon your hair, and only upon your hair. As a rule girls take one brush and go over each other's scalps, thereby contaminating all the scalps; carrying oily matter from head to head. The scalp of a blonde-haired girl is not kept in good condition by the same quality or amount of secretions that a brunette requires; a woman's scalp that has been neglected will carry to a young woman's sensitive skin germs which will affect her scalp and complexion, but would not probably affect a middle-aged person. So let no person use your brush and allow no other person's brush used upon you.

The habit of promiscuously kissing each other that some girls at this age of puberty so often have, is a dangerous habit, because you may have placed upon your lips some of the germs which cause pimples, and then comes trouble again. Anyway, a girl is too young to be kissed and not old enough to kiss—without danger to herself.

There are many, many more little things which cause a poor complexion in the girl and grown woman. First of all is that curse of American girls and women—constipation—the result of our false and injurious prudery. I warned you we should have to refer to it again and again, for it is a condition that enters into the cause of many women's illnesses, indispositions, tumors, open sores, headaches and other avoidable troubles.

Allowing any of the cast-off material of the stomach and intestines to remain in the lower bowel will most positively cause a muddy and pimpled skin. The reason is plain. This material is dead stuff meant to be cast off out of the body EVERY day. If it remains in the body it putrefies, forms gases and acids, which are REabsorbed into your system, taken up by the blood, which later on shows it in your face. Just think of it! Would you like to go around with all the signs of putrid matter being kept in your body? Of course not; yet you will outwardly show these signs if you do not keep your lower bowels always cleaned.

What is the best way to keep the bowels clean?

Regularity in your habits of toilet is, first of all, the most important factor. Drinking plenty of water—you see I am at it again—in the morning, is next in importance. Your breakfast food can be so arranged that the bowels will empty themselves every morning if the habit and water drinking have been carefully looked after. Fruit, stewed or ripe, should be taken every morning. Little or no meat is needed nor advisable for you in the morning. Cereals—real cereals, not the sawdust and roasted bread crust stuff—are good for the morning meal. Plain, old-fashioned oatmeal comes first, then hominy or similar cereals.

The idea that buckwheat or other breakfast cakes cause pimples is all nonsense. The same is true about syrups, butter or sugar. If you have flushed your stomach and intestines with water and fruit, you may eat all the cakes and sugar you wish. Candy does not affect your complexion, neither do cakes, pie, nor any sweets which ARE PURE AND EATEN AT THE PROPER TIME.

All our grandmothers' scare and advice about eating candy and other sweets is due to the fact that they DO harm in this way. Candy and other sweets are too often eaten between meals or early in the morning and thus cause a lack of appetite. With this loss of appetite, the body cannot get its nourishing and bowel-cleansing food. It is the loss of this nourishing food and the natural result of having nothing in the intestines which will wash these food tracts out, that does all the harm. It is living unnaturally to be in such a condition, and any unnatural way of living will bring about unhealth, and this will be shown by a poor and nasty-looking complexion, a hot skin and flabby flesh.

Young women and girls often need sugar in their system and at certain times will crave it. Other girls will crave something sour—pickles, for instance. EAT PICKLES AND CANDY IF YOU CRAVE THEM. But do not forget that first you must have had a breakfast free from these substances, have thoroughly emptied your bowels and had a good noon meal. After these good meals you may eat candy, pickles, ice cream, any old thing—IF THE MATERIALS ARE PURE. This is a very important matter. Eat nothing that has been exposed to the dust of the streets or any filthy place. We shall have something to say about "dope" drops and candies in which are brandies, cocaine and other drugs.

The girl who goes out at noon and buys for her luncheon éclaires, doughnuts, cream puffs and other pastry, and makes a meal of this stuff, is positively going to have a pasty complexion, be constantly constipated and unable to do her full amount of work—school, house or office. If she has taken some good soup and eaten a little nourishing food, THEN the pastry will not harm her; perhaps do her good.

I have said nothing about eggs or fish. I think most of you are glad of it and know the reason. I have had thousands of girls and young women under my charge and but few of them could eat either eggs or fish; and to many, milk was positively repulsive. At certain times these kinds of foods are nauseating to many girls and young women. Now and then a young woman will take an egg or a few bites of fish, but all through the active portion of her life she abhors a diet of such eatables. It is a case of—

Jack Spratt could eat no pie,
His wife could eat no fish;
So betwixt them both
Each had a separate dish.

Do not force yourself to eat anything that you do not enjoy. In good health the body will know what it needs. If it needs sugar, it will give you a craving for sugar; if you need beef, you will want it. The cravings for sweets or sours only become unnatural when they are eaten to the exclusion of nourishing food. If you have the HABIT of eating sweets in the morning, you must break this habit. You got into the habit because you gave in to a natural desire at an unnatural time.

If you are hungry before going to bed, then you will benefit by taking some nourishing and easily-digested food. Eating at night will NOT injure your complexion. It is eating indigestible food which ruins the complexion, and before bedtime you are too apt to eat those foods which lie all night in your stomach and ferment there. This is a sure and quick way to bring on a muddy complexion and a red nose.

Never drink milk with beef, pork or ham. But I do not fear this tough combination in girls or women, only it is best that you should know that such a combination will remain all night in your stomach and let you know it for a few days afterwards.

I know that the majority of girls and women who are out in the selfish world, including schoolgirls, do not fully realize the great importance of proper food eaten at the proper time, that is, the bearing it has upon all their growing powers. If they did, we should not have all these patent medicines for skin, womb, stomach, headaches, and all the other doped stuff, which is ruining hundreds of thousands of those who ought to be the mothers of the future generation. I say ought to be, because unless you girls take hold at once and absorb these facts I have been telling you, and shall tell you, many, yes, most of you, will weep throughout a childless life.

What shall I apply to my face?

Nothing but water and pure soap.

Does not washing the face in water, hot or cold, bring on wrinkles?

No, never. Did you ever see wrinkles upon your canary bird? Don't you have a bath ready for her every morning? What made the Greek and Roman maidens so beautiful in face, figure and complexion? Baths, bathing their bodies and faces daily.

But they used facial ointments, powders and creams. No, not the pure maidens or matrons; only the other kind.

If a woman, when young, was foolish or ignorant enough to use powder or grease upon her face and kept it up, when she gets to be thirty-five or so, she has to resort to enameling her face. If now she allowed her face to be thoroughly washed by either cold or warm water, she would have wrinkles, big, deep ones. She, of course, does not believe in water on the face and will tell you so; she has her reason. And the reason is this: For years she has been maltreating her skin by stopping the natural oil from leaving the skin glands. As time went on she has applied the necessary powder—necessary to her—then had to use some form of facial cream, increasing the amount year by year. There has been no opportunity for the skin to stretch or relax, to work out its secretions, it remains almost immovable; consequently ridges and furrows form, and a good wash brings out the wrinkles and also her secret.

There is no harm in having the face massaged when you are tired, dusty and your skin feels tightly stretched. But having it gently rubbed and washed with cold water, then protected by a veil as you go out into the fresh air, is an entirely different matter from having it rubbed by one who fills in the open pores with a "facial cream" or some "beautifier." There is only one beautifier, and that is GOOD HEALTH. And once you get it you do not have to apply it every day. It will stand the rain and the sun, will defy heat and salt sprays, will be always by your side wherever you go and not put you in the awful condition of a well-known professional beauty I once knew.

This woman was traveling and became ill. I was sent for, but when I arrived I was told by the maid that Madame could not see me at that hour. Now the case was important; the woman was suffering and in danger. Never mind, she simply COULD NOT see me for several hours. She went into a delirium and was finally taken to a hospital for mental invalids.

Why wouldn't she see me? Because her fine and notorious complexion had been left behind, and as the suffering from her pain had caused her to freely perspire, the perspiration had opened up all her wrinkles and furrows.

Unless the skin of the whole body is freely washed, the neglect will show on the complexion. A bath every morning is the secret of many bright and rosy cheeks. If you are so situated that you cannot get a tub bath every morning, winter and summer, you certainly can get a big sponge and have a sponge bath in your room. Let the water run down your spine, especially down the small of your back. Give your face a good dose of cold water. A shower on the face will keep wrinkles away until late in life. Do not stop your bathing because you are unwell, only use warm or tepid water. I know that many girls are told not to even put their hands in cold water while menstruating. This is utter nonsense, if the girl is otherwise in good health. These old ideas have done much harm and kept girls from benefiting themselves by helping Nature in all her growths.

Cold baths will keep your flesh firm and hard; will take off fat if you are too fat, and put on flesh if you are too lean. Like everything in nature, the improvement comes slowly, but it certainly comes. You should commence the baths in the summer and keep them up so that when the cold weather comes the change is not very noticeable. Of course all this should be done in a warm room and you should have a warm rug to stand upon. Be sure to take a good rub with a coarse towel.

This brings us to some simple form of exercise you can do at this time which will help the bowels to empty themselves by toning the muscles of the abdomen—the stomach, you call it.

These exercises consist in bending the body from your waist several times, then swinging from side to side. You do this with your feet close together and with straightened knees. Bend forwards and downwards, touching the floor with the tips of your fingers without bending the knees. Keep it up until you can do it without effort. Then swing your body from side to side, twisting and turning from the hips. Nothing will give you a more graceful figure than these forms of movements. Keep up this exercise all through your active life, and with all the other advice I have and shall give you, you can be attractive even when the gray hairs have made their appearance.

It is not the purpose of these Chats to advise you in purely medical matters, that is to tell you what to do in illness and what medicines to take. The purpose of these talks is to put you in possession of knowledge that will bring you to full womanhood, a strong, healthy woman to whom marriage and children will be a state of happiness for both husband and wife, or to a state of content, if you choose "single blessedness." But in the matter of constipation, I think it will do no harm to tell you that, if you will take once a week a tablespoonful of SODIUM PHOSPHATE, you will be benefited. This sodium phosphate should be taken before breakfast in a full glass of water.

What about thin hair, split hairs, that dead-feeling hair?

If this condition is found in the young woman, it is ninety-nine times out of a hundred her own fault, or due to her ignorance of what the scalp and hair need.

It is because she has piled a lot of dead and often diseased hair on top of her healthy and growing hair. Put a bunch of dead matter upon live and growing matter and what is the result? Death, decay!

Most of the fashions in hair and dress originate in those whose lives and age compel some artificial aid to attract attention. These foolish and freakish fashions are not for the young woman to adopt. Take the fashion of long trains, for example. The women of Paris seldom walk, they go about in automobiles or carriages. Now, sitting in these open conveyances it attracts attention to have a long folding train wrapped around the sitting figure and pulled up at the ankles to show a dainty slipper and silken hosiery. Don't you see how ridiculous it is for a good young woman who has to walk to her daily work or school, to try to copy a fashion which is intended for an entirely different class of women? Yet, when trains were the fashion, you all did it.

You are doing about the same foolish thing now with your head. Head-gear—that is the best name for it—is intended for women whose age has depleted them of much hair or whose lives have been such that their hair has become dead through bleaching or other injurious processes—these women must repair the damage. Wigs are too evident, so these women buy the hair which once graced or disgraced some other women, and pile it up in freakish forms and call it the latest fashion. The American girl and young woman immediately follow "the fashion," and then you ask me what to do for thin hair and dead tresses!

Now, if you keep up this heathenish fashion of ruining your own beautiful hair, many of you will not only have thin hair, but become BALDHEADED. False hair, such as "puffs," "rats," frames, pads, "transformations," "pin curls" and "mouse-traps," will do the trick for you. Even the artificial means used to puff out the natural hair will ultimately injure it—injure it beyond repair.

All the false hair with the appliances to keep it in shape, press on the scalp and impede the circulation of the blood, and the part of the scalp it should supply will wither and lose all life. The result of any pressure on the blood vessels of the scalp is that the roots of the hair become impoverished, and in time the hair gets so thin and weak that it drops out.

Very little, if any, air can get to the scalp when you are "following the fashion," which is just now in vogue. Stop this injurious and ridiculous wearing of false puffs, pads, and especially "transformations."

I have seen schoolgirls and typists with enough rigging of false hair and rusty wires upon their heads to give a strong man a constant headache and make him bald in a month. Your hair also falls out rapidly and constantly, but as you are blessed at the start with more luxuriant and more active growth in the scalp, it takes longer for the injury to show. But it is only a matter of time, not effect.

Then there is another matter which you do not fully realize—all good and worthy men detest this ill-smelling and dead hair you pile upon your heads. You lose all your fresh appearance, all the looks of a maiden, all the proofs of innocence. Your complexion takes on the hue of the dead hair, and when the fashion passes you can never get back the shining, luxuriant tresses men so dearly admire. Men and youths may not have told you these truths, but way down in their hearts they will pick a girl for a wife or sweetheart who has not the smell of a dead Chinaman, or whose hair has been the abiding place for an old "mouse-trap" and left the mousy odors.

The best way to insure a good head of hair is to wear it loose and free, without any artificial aids and appliances. Of course you may dress it any way it pleases you, but aside from pins it should never have any other pressure upon it.

The hair should be washed frequently in water with a little powdered borax, but remember you wash the hair only to clean the scalp, nothing should be applied to the hair directly.

There is another fashion which has made many a girl suffer from headaches, thinned her hair and injured her complexion. This is the wearing of tight collars, neck bands, and those torturing things with points you wear stuck right up under the ears. I forget now what you call them, and I won't tell you what I call them, for it would not sound nice to polite ears. But if you keep on wearing them a man will be able to say almost anything without you being able to hear him; for you will be deaf.

The reason these tight collars do so much injury is that they compress the arteries and veins of the neck, which at this part of the body are near the surface. They are large, full-blooded vessels and bring the blood to and return it from brain and scalp. I have known girls to faint simply from the compression due to tight collars or bands around the neck. They will almost invariably cause headaches, and every one of you know of the great relief you derive from taking them off and putting on a loose wrap or dressing sack. I have known women to suffer violent pains in the head, then dizziness and final collapse, by preventing a free circulation through the brain. The same blood vessels supply the skin, and when these are stopped from nourishing the skin what do you get? A poor, pale and finally diseased skin, a starved face.

Chapter V

Nerves and the Nervous Girl

It seems that not anything worth while in this world is gained without self-fighting and worry. The great things that are accomplished by men and women are accomplished only through will power, determination and concentration. Determination is different from will power in this respect: one may be determined to do a thing but find that she has not the nervous power to carry out the determination. In other words, the nervous force is really the basis of all will power. So all the factors which go to make for self-control and concentration upon whatever you have decided upon doing, are dependent upon a good and perfectly adjusted nervous system. Without a powerful nervous force we would be nothing but eating and sleeping animals.

The men and women who do not know from any personal feeling that there is a tremendous force in a trained nervous system are those who do nothing for the world's progress; they only eat, sleep and automatically labor. Many who have plenty of nervous force but do not know what it means, and hence cannot control it and use it for the benefit of man and themselves, are those who throw it away in dissipations, abnormal excitement and riotous living.

To have a highly-sensitive nervous organization is the greatest gift a woman can have; but unless she early knows its value and how to train it, it becomes a curse to her. It will run away with all her impulses—good and bad—and finally separate her from her womanly stability.

We hear a lot about "nervous women and girls;" and that the condition is increasing, due to our rapid way of living and all the pressure of trying to keep up the pace civilization has set. I have lived most of my life among nervous women and girls, and have come to the conclusion that the truth of the matter is, that instead of being due to our rapid pace of living and working, it is really due to the fact that most girls have never been taught to train and control their nervous forces.

These nervous girls and women are mostly those who are not over-nervous, but simply never have developed a nervous force that could keep pace with their physical and emotional activities. It is for this reason that their impulses get the better of them, they crave abnormal excitements, want to be on the go constantly, cannot be contented with simple and honorable home duties and finally merge into a condition where they have to seek the doctor or else go to a sanitarium.

Now just consider for a moment some simple facts. You are taught, early in life, the necessity of exercising in order to develop and be able to control your muscles. You are told to "learn to control your temper," but unless you are in perfect physical condition, with plenty of reserve nervous force, which is really will force, to use when you need it most, how are you to "control your temper"?

I have tried to tell you how necessary it is that all your organs should be kept in perfect condition by knowing what they are, and what they do and how to help them in doing the right thing. Your teachers are constantly at you to make you train your memory, to keep your mind upon your studies, or else your employer is nagging you to pay more attention to what you are told. And how many of you try to do all this and do not succeed!

"Train every faculty, build up your abilities;" do this or don't do that; always something is dinned into your ears about what you should do to improve yourself. But the one force, THE power which is at the bottom of every impulse or act, nerve activity, is left unmentioned as a force to be trained first, always and last of all the forces in your body.

"She has such a bad temper" is a remark we hear time after time. "If she would only learn to control her outbreaks; don't get out of temper," and similar expressions are only too frequently heard in homes and at school—everywhere. No wonder the helpless girl becomes discouraged and disgusted when she is scolded for petty explosions which she would gladly know how to stop.

A girl without a temper doesn't amount to much. It is a proper attitude of revolt against personal wrong or injustice. It is the birthright of every normal woman. It belongs to her protective instincts. And what is temper? Just the explosion of a highly nervous temperament. Explosion, mind you, not a decent expression of righteous indignation. The difference is that one is uncontrolled nervous force, the other is the same expression of nervous force held in check, governed by long training and handled for some forthright deeds. It is the preserving of this nervous force so as to be able to utilize it for some valuable work, that makes the difference between wasted energy and useless efforts and applied energy with useful results.

The nervous force in woman, including the brain, is the last to become fully developed, but it should be the first to be considered in your training. It means self-control, and there is no better evidence of good birth, well-poised personality and perfect physical health, than control over one's impulses and words.

A girl with these qualities will soon get a husband who will be kept as a husband.

To get self-control you must go at it in the same systematic manner as you do physical exercise. In this latter matter schools and clubs have gymnasiums for you; there are athletic games played under instructors of physical culture who teach you how to exercise along lines which will give you good bodily health; but the apparatus you need first of all, that for building and strengthening the nervous system and the nervous energy which goes into your sex development, are merely mentioned in some homes and schools and in some others never mentioned. You need a perfectly-balanced nervous organization and one under your complete control before you can benefit from any physical exercise.

"But," you say, "is not physical exercise a means of building up the nervous organization?"

No, only indirectly. This body of ours, the mere bones, muscles and organs, is only the frame of our human machine, just as the steel body and wheels are that of an automobile. No matter how strong that frame is, no matter what fine material has gone into the workmanship, it is absolutely worthless unless the motor which is to drive it is powerful enough to send it along with ease, and moreover be one which can readily and safely always run under control.

The motor that runs our bodies is the nervous system, and if you have a body so highly developed as to fatigue the nervous motor, then a nervous breakdown is certain to occur. If you have a nervous mechanism too strong for the body it will run away with you and then we have another kind of "nervous breakdown"—hysteria, melancholy, insomnia, drug habit or worse.

The nervous affections of girls and women are generally due to one of these causes I have outlined—unevenness in bodily development or nervous development. They should balance each other, work together and both become tired and demand rest at the same time.

The secretions of the skin, kidneys, liver and other internal organs are controlled through the nervous system. So are the functions of the womb, ovaries and even the heart. Why does your heart beat so rapidly after a fright or great excitement? Because your nervous motor is running beyond your control. Why does a girl's monthly occurrence sometimes stop after a great fright or skip a period or two during some deep grief or emotional experience? Because the nervous organization of the whole body was put to excessive work and then had to stop for a rest. Having become temporarily exhausted the fine little nerve endings in the organs cannot do their allotted work, hence no secretions can push their way out of the closed cells. For these nerve fibers open and close the cells which secrete the materials that should be cast off at regular intervals.

Not being able to do so the girl becomes "tired," has headaches, feels "all out of sorts." Then she thinks something is wrong with her, her good mother gives her "tonics" or "blood medicine" and she is told to exercise.

What she needs instead of exercise or medicines is rest; as much rest and food as she can contentedly stand. The only exercise such a condition calls for is deep breathing and this more to furnish fresh blood which the full lungs give, than for the exercise itself. If we could conveniently get fresh air into the lungs by some method other than breathing it, it would be better still, for even the effort of deep breathing calls for some use of the nervous force, and the least possible disturbance of this force, the quicker will the girl or woman recover her full nervous strength.

If you have exercised beyond the power of the nervous system to send full impulses to the skin so that it will pour out its poisons, some of this poison remains in the body and sets up a condition known as auto-intoxication, which only means self-poisoning. All kinds of nervous affections arise from this state.

The same conditions are brought about by the poisons of the liver, if the delicate nerves of this big sewer of the body are too tired to open up all the little ducts and channels and let out the poisons which the liver has taken up from the blood in your body. And so we might go on into more physiology, showing you that much of the nervousness among girls comes from over-exercise, instead of under-exercise. Probably more of the trouble arises from exercising at wrong times; at times when the nervous organization has all it can do to regulate sex growth and development of the girl. At this time to pull out a lot of nervous power to make muscles work and grow big, must result in some nervous organ being deprived of its needed nerve cell assistance.

In these facts lies the cause for so many nervous wrecks in young women and wives. Nature gives the nervous system of all growing girls constant and concentrating work to do. It has to take care of all the new organs of secretions, see that the breasts are fully supplied with cells ready to do their work when motherhood approaches, fit its tiny but powerful nerve endings to the womb and ovaries, develop the brain and instincts along proper and healthful lines, furnish power to the million cells of the scalp and skin, watch that the stomach pours out a proper amount of digestive fluid at a time when the girl has a craving for strange "eatables" such as slate pencils or gum arabic. The hard and enduring efforts of the nervous system to keep the girl well balanced in her thoughts all the time she is undergoing these necessary changes, should never be overlooked.

No girl between fourteen and twenty years of age should ever train for physical contests or any form of athletic competition. A girl should train for her future work—motherhood—and for this wonderful and glorious contest for bringing onto the earth the best possible men and women, she must have the highest form of nervous development, with all that this implies.

The best way to help all this effort of Nature to give you a nervous system which will stay by you when the worries and trials of life come, is never to over-exercise at any time, and not to exercise at all for a few days before and a few days after your periods. This is the time when your body needs all the reserve power for one purpose.

How can I tell when I need rest instead of exercise?

The best sign is when you think that you ought to exercise but don't feel like making the effort. Many, many a girl has become a nervous wreck because someone forced her to exercise when she needed to be quiet and at rest.

Never exercise unless the anticipation of the play or game is a pleasure to you. When you get into that state of mind such as, "Oh, I don't feel like making the effort; I'd rather sit here and read, or talk"—if you feel like that, if you have to make up your mind that you must exercise, but it is difficult to find any pleasure in the thing you are thinking of doing; don't try to do it.

If you make determined efforts to do any physical work that is distasteful to you, if you work by the clock, then you are injuring yourself every minute you are at it. You are drawing upon your nervous capital, not upon the interest. This is the secret of all exercise, brain or muscle: work must be done upon saved-up interest, not upon the capital. If you use the capital, it only means for the body what it would mean for the purse—bankruptcy—sure and certain failure.

Any physical effort which leaves you feeling worse than when you started, is injuring you. This does not mean a good physically tired feeling, one in which your cheeks are aglow, when you feel elated at what you have done, when a cold shower bath feels good instead of making you shiver and covered with "gooseflesh," but that feeling of complete exhaustion, pale cheeks, a feeling of shivering if cold baths are mentioned and a longing for something to drink that will brace you up. When this latter state is yours, you have over-exercised or else exercised at a time when your nervous motor needed a rest, not disturbance.

You sometimes hear it said, "Why, she is the last girl in the world I thought would ever get nervous troubles. She is the best girl on the team—Oh! you ought to see her muscles."

Yes, but you should also see those worn-out nerve cells.

Misdirected ambition, a forgetfulness that she had only a certain amount of nervous power, an excitement which blinded her to her real condition; these were the factors which made her drive her motor far beyond its powers. Finally there was no more nervous energy to move her over-developed muscles without fatigue, and fatigue has its own poisons which penetrate the whole body and then comes a collapse. This was the cause for this "strong girl's" nervous breakdown.

No girl is strong, or ever will be as a woman, whose body and muscles have been developed at the expense of her nervous system. The really strong girl is one who has power saved up, and when a time of great stress or work comes, has this extra power to put out and not become a nervous bankrupt.

Exercise, like your daily work, should always be a pleasure instead of boresome labor. Only by doing things in this state of mind can you ever be successful.

The drilling, training and developing of the will—powers of self-control—must be a constant part of a girl's self-education. It is all very well to tell a girl to "use will power," but before she is blamed for the lack of control, it would be only just to her to find out just how much of this power she has to use.

Will power depends upon a perfect nervous system. The reason one cannot call to a will power to stop an evil or disagreeable habit, is because the habit has temporarily destroyed, or rather put to sleep, the power to will. If there has not been, in the beginning, a well-drilled self-control—or will power—how can you expect a girl who flies off into an unreasonable temper, to immediately control this temper and keep it under control?

The will power is the rudder of life; the steering control over our human ship as it voyages on the seas of life. Now if a ship should go to sea without a rudder, you know just what would happen to it. If it goes on a voyage with a weak rudder, or one which has been damaged and not repaired, the best sailor in the world cannot keep it off the rocks when a storm comes.

It is just so with our brains and bodies; they must be controlled by a strong and well-attached rudder, the will power. With such a power one can accomplish wonders; in fact, everything that seems marvelous to us in man's work has been due to perfect steering of right impulses into new harbors where an unsteady human ship would be wrecked in trying to pass the hidden rocks and roaring reefs.

Chapter VI

How to Get Will Power

But just what must one do to get this power?

I have told you something about the body's poisons, how they accumulate in the body and cause illness and nervousness. The first thing to do is to see that your body is free and kept free from these poisons, for if not kept free, the nerve cells become affected and then a perfect will power cannot be developed.

Here are a few practical things to do and not to do to keep the nerve cells so you can develop them. Sleep always alone. Sleeping with another person is unsanitary. The skin needs to get rid of its natural poisons and not take up any from another person. You would not think of breathing the air coming from another person's lungs. Well, when you are under the sheets and blankets with another person, you can breathe through your skin the poisons coming from this companion. If you have to sleep in a room with another person, you must have your own little bed. Sleep with as little covering over you as is possible with comfort; window, of course, as I have warned you, wide open at the top. You can become accustomed to lighter clothing by gradual methods of reducing the number of blankets.

No underclothing of a material to absorb and retain perspiration should ever be worn. If you keep over your skin any clothing which has become moist through perspiration it will injure your chances of keeping a good nervous force. Take off such clothing before it becomes soggy and cold.

Then take a sponge bath and put on dry clothing.

Personally, I believe that porous linen underwear is the best for all growing girls—yes, and for all women. It allows a free evaporation of perspiration, and so prevents a more or less sodden garment from remaining in contact with the skin, which so frequently happens with those who wear woolen underclothing. There is another harmful effect that woolen underclothing is apt to have; the beginning of a rheumatic condition which later on in life becomes a painful chronic rheumatism.

In girls who find that in winter linen underwear is too cold, a thin silk vest may be worn over the linen. This will be found to constitute a thoroughly warm, comfortable and safe form of underwear.

Don't try to keep awake either by mental effort or that injurious resort of drinking coffee. Sleepiness should not be overcome as a rule, as it is Nature's signal to stop work. In fact, Nature has signals for almost all dangers, and when we can read these signals all goes well along the road of life.

If efforts are continued in spite of the fatigue, the quality of the work is poor and the exhaustion to your nervous system will be difficult to repair. High-school girls and college young women constantly make this error and then wonder why they become so nervous at times. All sorts of things are tried to keep awake in order to study or dance, when if they would go to bed and rest, they could accomplish far more in half the time in the morning with little or no fatigue. For remember, I am trying to tell you how to get a grip upon that will power.

Yet there are times when sleepiness and fatigue must be overcome without resort to stimulants which will surely weaken any will power you may have been cultivating. These times are when you have to watch by the bedside of an ill mother or someone dear to you. When so situated, go to an open window and take deep breathing exercises. This will burn up the fatigue poisons in your body, for remember these poisons are gathering in everyone's body when real fatigue commences.

Morning is the time for all mental work if you are a high-school girl or college woman. The afternoon should be devoted to some form of mild exercise and for "low pressure" work.

Shouting, yelling and all extra efforts of the throat muscles will aid in exhausting your nervous powers, to say nothing about the unpleasant and unladylike attitude it places you in before the public. A low, sweet voice, even under excitement, is a sound pleasing to all men and a certain mark of good birth.

I need not repeat the facts about the advertised "remedies" for this trouble or that pain, for I have already warned you to let all drugs and "cures" alone as you would snakes. But there are some drinks that you should be warned against. Never take those soda water fountain's stuff advertised as "nerve tonics." Don't believe the young man or boy at the fountain when he says that "Dopie" or "Bromo Tonic," "Phosphate for your Nerves," or "Dockine" and other similar rotten stuff will do you good and that they contain no drugs or injurious materials. Don't believe a word of all these misleading statements. The boy or young man is there to sell, not to understand or care about your condition.

If such stomach wash and nerve destroyers contain no drugs, then what good are they? If they contain nothing but plain water charged with carbonic acid gas, then why not take a glass of plain seltzer or soda water? Supposing, for example, these advertised drinks do not contain harmful drugs—most of them do, however—they are colored and sweetened. What are they colored with? What is the chemical that sweetens them? If you really knew you would be unable to keep them down, the knowledge of how they are concocted would be revolting to you.

These restrictions do not apply to pure soda water and pure syrups, but even here you must be careful to drink only those which are pure, and only the very best drug stores are safe in this matter.

Most of the bottled drinks sold at five cents should be thrown into the sewers, and how many diseased lips do you think have touched the glasses passed around at the circus and similar shows? Those glasses containing dyed water, a little chemical acid and glucose, with second-hand lemon peel to give the appearance of lemonade, are almost as dangerous as the fangs of a viper.

Don't dress in a loud and gaudy manner unless you wish to attract the men of loud and loose principles. The personal appearance of a girl makes a great difference in the manner she will be received. To dress in good taste and with every appearance of neatness and modesty, is essential for the girl who seeks employment or respectful attentions. Good taste in dressing simply means that a man can say that the girl was well dressed, but to save his life he could not tell just what she had on for clothes or hat. The dressing of the feet is, perhaps, the first thing a refined and cultivated man looks at. To be well and sensibly shod is always a hall mark of good birth and cultivation. The girl who wears thin shoes on a wet and cold day, the young woman who displays high-heeled shoes and thin silk stockings on a winter's day, may attract attention, but not respect. A man well knows that if a girl wears a fur coat and low shoes on the street, she will, as a wife, be continually complaining of her indisposition, pains and altogether make his home a place to flee.

No man wants a nervous and complaining woman around his house, and a girl who thinks she is attractive on the street is not the girl who will be attractive in a home. That is, one who dresses her feet for the street in the manner they should be dressed for the house or ballroom proclaims herself a careless girl and one who is not liable to take care of her health.

You have heard much about psychotherapy, suggestion and a lot about certain Movements in church circles. These all proclaim an infallible remedy for "Nerves." There is a lot of nonsense written about this mental method of healing the nervous and soul-sick person, and, on the other hand, there has been a lot of scoffing at it. There is more in the drilling of our inner selves than the old-time physician has been willing to admit; he has so long been accustomed to consider woman a physical being of bones, flesh and whims, that her real inner self has been sadly neglected. The consequence has been that a number of well-meaning and progressive men have taken up the treatment of troubles without understanding just what relation the gross bodily organs and nerve cells bear to this inner self which we all possess. I shall not bother you with any digression, but get at once to what you can do for yourselves in this matter.

Start early to get inside of yourself; to get at that self which so bothers you at times; the thing which makes you "feel out of sorts," that "getting mad with yourself;" the feeling that you have not said or done just what you would like to have said or done, but which some uncontrollable impulse, at the moment, made you say and do. This is the inner self, but it belongs to all the other parts of your body; is really the best part of you and will be able to put out the best in you when you have it under full control.

Take a half hour at the time when you can be alone and see into yourself. Search well your heart and learn just what you said or did that you regret. Then find out what caused you to be disagreeable, what has put you out with your better self. Write these thoughts and desires down where you can privately refer to them daily. Take the first mistake and stick to the memory of it so that, when the impulse comes to repeat it, you can check yourself. Drilling yourself this way, you will soon learn to conquer this one fault. Then start in the same way at another fault and conquer that. Don't try to exercise all the powers of resistance at once, for if you do, there are bound to be failures and too many of these make for discouragement, and then follows recklessness. You would not try to develop a weak back by going from an apparatus meant to develop the thighs to another one for the chest, and then back again for a few moments to that for strengthening the back muscles. No, you stick to the work which develops the back until you have made some decided progress. The inner self, the will, the good girl in you, should be developed in the same way.

You want to go to a dance or perhaps the theater, "all the other girls are going," but your mother has good and sufficient reasons for not allowing you to go. Now, instead of arguing, complaining and going off to your room in a huff, saying unkind words to your good mother, words which tear and gnaw at her heart, speak to that inner self; call it out; go to your room and peer straight into the trouble with YOU, not that wrong idea that the fault is with your mother.

Think deeply of this fact; she is your mother, nothing that would add to your pleasure or advantage would she deprive you of—not for an instant. But as your mother she knows what is best for you; she may know something about the other girls, about the kind of youths going with them, she may know something about your health that is not advisable to tell you just at the moment. In your room think all these matters over; throw out that unreasonable and false self, and when you have done so, go to your mother, ask her forgiveness and also beg her to tell you her reasons.

Now that your inner self is in control, your mother will tell you confidentially her reasons, and when they are clear to you, the happiness which follows is far beyond any mere physical pleasure you can ever obtain. After a few times of this self-drilling, the obedience to your mother will be a second nature.

Still more fights with your inner self will have to follow, but one by one, you can conquer the enemy. Never become discouraged if you fail, just keep on trying and in the end you will win over all evil and wrong impulses.

A girl who disobeys her mother or father is the girl who as a wife will be divorced.

The girl who wants to "be a good Indian" will, when a woman, be a repulsive savage.

The girl who deceives her mother will deceive her husband.

All men know this fact.

Remember that marriage does not make a happy woman, but a woman has it in her power to make marriage a happiness.

The most reasonable woman will have hours of being unreasonable, but these are the hours you should be unreasonable with yourself while searching for reasons.

Chapter VII

How to Keep Attractive

The jolly, vivacious girl; the girl who is happy obeying her mother, contented in school or laughs while at work, is really a girl in whom every organ and function are properly adjusted. In other words, a girl who is in perfect health is a joy to herself and makes life worth living for others. It is the same idea that I have given you regarding a perfectly-running machine—every part works harmoniously and there is no complaining, no feeling of harshness in life, no grinding or jolting as you go along.

And almost every girl who starts right can be put in this desired state and keep herself so. But she must understand that it is in her own power to have red cheeks, happy thoughts, vivacity, pleasure in what she does, and to bring sunshine around her.

Doctors cannot do this for her; patent medicines, "blood purifiers," "eye drops," tonics and complexion foods; all and everything of the kind will injure her and prevent any chance of obtaining and keeping perfect health. I purposely repeat this statement, for we are now going to chat in detail about many of those little things you can do for yourself better than any doctor—even the most experienced. Of course you cannot do all this until you understand the causes for those many little annoyances which come to every growing girl.

Your complexion, your spirits, your physical form, all depend upon what the body takes in and what it casts off. This cannot too often be repeated to you, because the simple facts are so easily understood when clearly explained and are under the control of every girl.

It does make all the difference between a vivacious and attractive girl and one who is constantly complaining, who knows that her eyes and complexion are dull; how life appears to each; all the difference between happiness and misery. And this difference arises from the methods of eating, thinking, and getting rid of the body's poisons. One girl does not know that all the cells in her body are constantly undergoing decay and new ones taking their places and so neglects to give her body such food, rest and exercise as will keep the body's outgo and input evenly balanced. The other girl with red cheeks and laughing mouth, has this evenly balanced condition during the body's constant changes.

Too many of you have been taught to neglect the proper feeding process of the body; you have been allowed to eat proper food at improper times and not been shown the necessity of doing just the opposite. But few of you have ever considered the true relation of food to health and happiness; the fruit market has been neglected, the butcher disinterestedly visited and the greengrocer never considered as an aid to perfect health. What have taken their places? Patent medicines, all sorts of poisonous "tonics," drugs, fake foods and hundreds of dangerous concoctions to replace the want of real nourishment.

Instead of nourishing the body and of course the nerves, these fake foods directly injure every cell in the body. They cannot keep up the repair daily needed in every tissue of the human system. Do not forget that every day your body undergoes more or less wear. In the growing girl it is unstable, sometimes through much worry or fear the wear is greater than the ability to repair, and unless the girl realizes this and at once commences to give extra aid to the repairing process by eating proper food and plenty of it, resting from all physical and mental excitement, she will reach full womanhood with some little nerve or tissue lacking its full strength; and she can never repair the damage.

Each day, too, by radiation, her body loses a large amount of heat, and for the perfect health of man or woman the temperature of the body must be maintained. Now this loss of heat has to be replaced constantly. It is only done through the regular supply of fuel. This fuel is the food we eat. It must be of such a nature as to burn up in the body and give out its heat. This fuel—food—has to be supplied according to the amount of work the body and brains do every day—yes, every hour. If you have to keep the furnace going to warm your rooms, you well know that it must have good coal about so often; according to the amount of work it is compelled to do. You also know that putting clinkers, shavings or newspapers into the furnace will not give your rooms the needed heat. Well, it is just so with your body.

Also, if you allow the clinkers from good coal to remain in the bottom of the furnace, soon there comes a time when no amount of coal will give out the full strength of its heat, and finally the fire goes out. Again, it is just the same thing that happens if you keep the clinkers of your fuel in your body; the waste products left over after the food has given out its heat. You know how these waste products are eliminated from your body—through the bowels, skin, kidneys, lungs and liver.

Now, please remember this most important fact—Food, including water, is for the sole purpose of supplying heat to the body and to replace the dead cells which are constantly being cast off in every portion of your body. This decay and birth of the cells of the body goes on in every living thing. When the decay is greater than the repair, some part of your body is dying. In such a condition, you are a fit subject for the attack of some of the many disease germs all around us. It may be a serious one or merely some form of skin disease; then goes, whack! your good complexion.

A girl needs more food and at more frequent intervals than a grown woman because, besides keeping up the heat of the body she also has to supply the material for the growing process active in her. The building up of the frame, the full strength of the nerves, the hard working blood, must all be supplied by a surplus of food, for if she eats only enough to supply heat, the other needs of her body will suffer and finally become useless.

Now, girls, eat plenty of food that will aid in all your growth. I know some girls who think it is unladylike to have a good appetite; I have treated girls who were really starving themselves because they dreaded to become fat, and I have seen others whose appetite was unnatural because they denied themselves proper food. It is not necessary for me to say any more about the kind of foods to eat; we have already gone into this matter, but remember this, that the degree of energy essentially depends on the nutritiveness of the food you do eat.

Not a single gland in the body can do its proper work unless it is supplied with its proper stimulant; and this stimulant is food. If you wish to have a soft, smooth and attractive skin, you must always keep in your mind the fact that it is the glands of the skin that exist for this very purpose. I have said something to you about perspiration and exercise, but beside this activity of the glands, produced by exercise, there is constantly an "insensible perspiration" taking place in every girl.

This unnoticeable perspiration amounts daily to about two pints of watery fluid. Think of it! A quart of water leaving your body through the skin every twenty-four hours and in such a way that you do not notice it. You see now why I have laid so much stress upon the statement that you should drink plenty of water, and why the average American girl suffers from poor complexion and constipation.

Fat is poured out in this "insensible perspiration." Even the finger tips will secrete it. If the palm of the hand is cleansed with soap and then with ether; held in the sunlight and observed with a magnifying glass, you can see little bubbles arising which immediately evaporate, leaving tiny drops of an oily substance—fat.

If this is so—and it is a scientific fact—is not the statement I made to you, that water will help reduce fat instead of making it, easily understood? But, then, why will drinking water also make fat? Because it simply balances the physiological functions, brings about a proper chemical action throughout the whole body and in doing this enables the tissues to extract from your food the elements which go to make up fat, flesh and blood.

In other words, give the body its needed supply of water, air, food and exercise, and it will take care of itself—give you the amount of fat you really need or take off the fat you do not need.

All these matters of controlling the action of the skin are dependent upon special nerves; nerves which have nothing to do but look after the health of the skin. These are the nerves which close or open the pores to let out the "insensible perspiration," which keep the body temperature equal under all conditions of exposure and rest, which allow the blood to get through the tiny arteries and veins of the cheeks and make for a good or poor complexion.

Don't listen to those who tell you that your unsatisfactory complexion is due to "bad blood." There is really no such state in the good girl or woman as "bad blood." Affections of the skin such as a muddy complexion, greasy looking skin, rough skin, pimples and blotches are not signs that there is something the matter with your blood. Generally speaking these are signs of some faulty adjustment between nerves and blood vessels, sweat glands and the tiny muscles of the skin.

These muscles of the skin are very delicate and sensitive muscles and easily prevented from working properly. When they do not do their work constantly and correctly, what happens? Wrinkles of course, then a tightening of the skin which prevents the outpour of the "insensible perspiration" and the escape of the oily substance. This latter, remaining, causes the greasy skin; the tiny wrinkles keep behind the outer skin some of the inward dirt, and then you have the muddy complexion.

Another way you can see the action of these tiny skin muscles is in "gooseflesh." "Gooseflesh" is due to the general contraction of these tiny skin muscles. They contract into the little pin-head knobs which make the peculiar appearance we call "gooseflesh." The contracting or expanding of these skin muscles is absolutely necessary for good health, as the action regulates secretion and excretion and also protects the body from sudden temperature changes. When you jump into bed and find the sheets cold, you immediately have "gooseflesh;" that is, the skin muscles close at once all the pores. If they did not do this, the contact with the cold sheets would reduce your body temperature and disturb the even working of the organs of the body. The reason fear and shock also bring on "gooseflesh" is due to the nerves of the skin being affected by the fright you have had, and so the muscles become uncontrollable. This causes the skin muscles to contract and its bunches are the "gooseflesh" skin. Very often a fright or emotion is the cause for a bad complexion, for as you can readily understand, all the functions of the skin being disturbed, it cannot remain healthy.

It is for this reason you should avoid all thoughts, reading or association which will affect the nervous system, if you wish to have a clear and beautiful complexion.

Proper clothing has, of course, a great deal to do with preventing a disturbance of the nerves of the skin and through these nerves the muscles of the skin. I have warned you about keeping next to your skin any garment soggy with human excretions or secretions—perspiration with its fats and acids—and explained why a daily bath is the only way to be certain of a healthy and hence a beautiful skin. The changing of underwear by a set rule—such as once or twice a week, is barbarous. Undergarments should be changed as often as they have absorbed any unusual amount of perspiration. Always change after exercise, and in the warm weather every day. It is not absolutely necessary that clothing worn during a morning's walk should be sent to the laundry, but it should be hung where it can dry, then put where the fresh air will go through its meshes. This being thoroughly done it may be used during the next form of exercise. But if it has been soaked with perspiration, then it should be thoroughly washed and dried in the air.

Carelessness in these matters is often the cause of skin diseases; especially of that distressing affection, eczema.

Woolen undergarments are a prolific source of mischief in most of these cases. In fact, as I have suggested to you, woolen underwear is not the thing for a girl or young woman to wear if she wishes a clear and attractive complexion.

Even in cold weather you can wear silk, muslin, or linen undergarments next the skin. Be certain to have them white, or at least undyed, and have no colored ribbons where they can come in contact with the skin. Outside of these garments you may wear woolen articles required for warmth. Another little matter of importance to the growing girl—fur, velvet or cloth collars of garments worn tightly about the neck, the lining of gloves, dyed stockings and even the lining of your hats, sometimes will start a skin trouble which will be difficult to cure.

Your sleeping garments should be as loose as possible—especially around the neck. They should be such that you can turn IN them and not have them stick to your body when turning.

Turning while in bed is one of Nature's ways of giving all the skin covering your body a chance to get air and allow of the evaporation of that "insensible perspiration." Now, if a certain part of your body has gotten rid of its inside poison—the region over the liver, for example—and in turning over to give that portion access to air, your garment simply sticks and goes with it, don't you see that you are sleeping with a soggy bit of clothing pasted right over the region which needs fresh air and a chance to evaporate its perspiration?

During warm weather you will find bran baths not only very soothing, but giving to the skin a very smooth and pleasing appearance. About four pounds of bran to a bathtub of water is what you need.

There is an annoying skin affection, though not a disease, which may embarrass the most careful girl. It is a summer occurrence and I dare say that most of you know something about it. I refer to "prickly heat," a most annoying thing to the girl who wishes to enjoy her summer outing and has to keep away from the bathing beach and the pleasures of all her friends. This trouble may come out suddenly all over the body, sometimes it is confined to certain large areas, more often to the arms and shoulders. It is accompanied by excessive sweating and intolerable itching, prickling and tingling.

You all can avoid this distressing condition. Light clothes, linen undergarments of the flimsiest material, the use of plenty of water taken inwardly, the avoidance of hot rooms, no exercise, such as dancing or tennis, are the things to remember.

Do not put anything on the skin such as powder, ointment or ammonia. Bathe in cool water; put into your bath a handful of bicarbonate of soda. Take every morning a full glass of some saline water or a glass of water in which you have dissolved a lithia tablet. Eat plenty of green vegetables and fresh fruit, but avoid spiced food. Rice, chicken, mutton, will not harm you, but pork, ham and underdone beef at this time should be let alone. At night you should sponge your body with vinegar and water.

Whatever affects the skin affects also the hair and nails, for those are only extensions of the skin. I have told you about the hair in a former chat which leaves little more to say; for after you understand the secret of beauty—good health—common-sense will dictate to you what to do. However, here are a few more things about the care of the hair.

In trying to get rid of some of the dirt which the hair will collect, don't use a fine tooth comb. This cannot, without difficulty and injury, be made to take hold of the dirt, because when it does, it will pull so severely as to pull out or break the hairs. This is especially true of the thick hair of the brunette. Use a comb having large smooth teeth. Your brush should have bristles moderately stiff and the tufts of these bristles should be well set apart. Never use a brush whose bristles are short and closely set. Pearline is a good washing material in which to soak your combs and brushes. In drying the brush be certain to place it in the sun, bristles down, so that the water drains off, instead of soaking into the back of the brush. If this latter condition is allowed, the moist roots of the bristles will take up all the dirt and germs floating around and they will then be transferred to your scalp.

The number of times the hair should be washed depends entirely upon the amount of dirt or dust it has accumulated. But the rule is, as I have mentioned, that washing the hair should be done only when there is an accumulation of dust, for the more it is let alone the better hair you will have. In washing the hair you remove the protective oil and this leaves the hair dry and brittle. All applications of oil or vaseline to the hair are injurious; man cannot make the artificial take the place of the natural. If you must use any oil, then use pure olive oil.

Never attempt to remove superfluous hair from the face or neck. If you do attempt it yourself, unsightly pimples will follow, perhaps ugly sores and in the end the roots will be left to send out larger and darker hairs. If troubled with superfluous hairs, go to a reputable physician. He can, by a method of using an electric needle, rid you of your trouble. Never go to an advertising man or woman for this trouble or any other.

Never try to beat Nature—you cannot do it. Help her and she will do the best thing for you. I make this remark because I know many girls who have straight hair want to have curly hair and try all kinds of methods to get curls.

Curly hair is due to the angle it is placed in the skin of the scalp. Straight hair simply means that the hair grows straight up from the scalp. You can now see that it is impossible to get a natural curly hair from straight roots. If you persist in this useless process, you are bound to disturb the roots and ultimately find that your hair is dropping out.

Then there is another fact to remember. The face and skin develop along their own lines and in harmony with each other. A face and complexion made for straight hair will always look somewhat out of proportion surrounded by artificially curled hair. This gives the head and face that "frowsy" look so often seen in the most carefully dressed girl. Such a girl thinks she has beaten Nature. But it is the other way about.

Don't use a HAIR nailbrush. In doing so you are liable to tear the tender skin at the base of the nails and open opportunities for germs. A rubber nail brush is the very best to use. Such a brush is generally called a flesh brush. It is a rubber plate with many cylindrical projections rising from one of its flat surfaces. These little rubber projections do better work than the bristles of a hairbrush and get in under the nail better and do much less damage. The flesh brush, beside cleaning the nails well, and with little damage to the surrounding skin, is itself easily washed and sterilized.

The finger nails ought to be trimmed so that they may fulfill their function of supporting and protecting the pulp of the fingers. They therefore ought to be cut in a line corresponding to, but slightly behind, the round of the finger tip. They should not be cut too close at the corners. The manicure method of cutting the nails close at the corners and trimming them too close, is injurious and dangerous. The finger nails can pick up more poisonous germs than any other portion of the body, and unless they are protected by their tough surroundings they will carry into the body deadly microbes. Never use a knife or nail scissors in pushing back the skin lying at the base of the nails. Gently work it back by the tip of your fingers or thumb.

Chapter VIII

Some Don'ts

Don't think because you hear so much about the dangerous germs to be found everywhere, that you are certain to catch some horrible disease. True, there is great danger in ignorantly living around these germs, but the danger is mostly in ignorance and not in the fact that the disease microbes are always with us.

The old idea that such germs as those of scarlet fever, typhoid, smallpox, etc., could be carried from the ill to the well on clothing, books, toys and other similar articles is not strictly true. Equally true is it that these kinds of germs do not stay long upon walls of rooms, floors or ceilings. They will stay and breed diseases in such places if they are allowed to thrive under moist and dark conditions.

Sunlight and fresh air are deadly enemies to all germs except those of venereal origin. If a smallpox patient has been confined to a room and after being taken away the room is fumigated and then closed, the chances are that the smallpox germs—some of them—will remain and increase. Hence, to again occupy this room would be dangerous. But if, instead of fumigating the room, if all the windows were open; if every corner and floor could receive the rays of the sun for many days; the last germ in the room would have to give up the ghost.

Don't think that fumigating and washing clothes or other articles which have come in contact with a diseased person make for absolute safety. But do remember that SUNLIGHT and fresh air are deadly enemies to most disease germs.

There are certain diseases which are carried around by persons in whom you would never suspect danger. Typhoid germs, for example, may be carried around in the intestines of a person who is in apparent health. Now everywhere this person lives, or uses the toilet, the germs are deposited, and if they happen to get into the drinking water—wells or streams—or are carried by the flies' legs to the food or milk, you run great risks of getting typhoid fever.

Those germs of two horrible diseases which are to be found upon public toilet articles, public drinking cups, upon the leaves of common books—in fact everywhere man or woman is to be found, are *not* killed by sunlight or fresh air. This subject should be thoroughly understood by every young woman, but it is of too great importance to be dealt with here in a few paragraphs.

The breath of a consumptive patient will not carry directly the germs of consumption to another person. Oh, I know that is what many of you have been taught, but we are dealing with the facts as they are known up to this very year of 1911. It has long been the general idea that disease germs were carried from one person or thing to another person or thing. Now this is not strictly true. All germs increase and thrive in moist and dark conditions. The throat of a consumptive patient is one of these conditions. The germs are sent out into the air of the room in surrounding moisture. They land somewhere; on the tablecloth, in the carpet, or hide in a dark corner. In these places they dry and become dust—germ-laden dust. Now stir up this dust and then you have the germs free to rush into the healthy lungs around them, and then a person runs great risk of contracting consumption.

Don't stir up a room by dusting if that room has been occupied by a diseased person. Don't wash the walls or floor of such a room and then close it, unless you want to go into the business of breeding germs.

Knock out the windows of such a room—open it up for the sun's rays to penetrate and kill off the enemy. Take all carpets out and put them where nothing but DRY air and sunshine can get at them. Do the same thing with every movable object in the room.

Don't do anything but just this with rooms where scarlet fever, diphtheria, measles, whooping cough and other contagious diseases have been running their courses.

I spoke to you about the hands being the greatest carriers of infection. They even carry around the germs of typhoid fever. They have been found on the cleanliest person's hands after using public toilets. On the fingers, especially.

You are safer in kissing a person who has consumption, than you are in wetting your finger to turn over the pages of a book that has been thumbed by scores of other persons. A person may have the cleanest habits possible yet be a menace to others as well as to herself.

I watched the other day a pair of young schoolgirls trying on each other's gloves. Up to the lips would go a finger or two, then these moist fingers would clasp the glove fingers and in this way work the glove onto the hand. You all know the process better than I can describe it to you. Now supposing that the girl who owned the glove had rang the bell or turned the knob at the residence of a friend who was ill with, say, consumption, to inquire how the friend was. Don't you see that it was more than probable that nurse, maid or mother had conveyed moist germs of the disease to the knob or bell push, that the germs dried but had not been long enough in the sun to be killed, and this girl's glove picked these germs up and then you transferred them to your lips? Dried germs which only wanted the moisture of your lips to become virulently active.

Don't wet your fingers in trying on gloves—new or old.

Don't hang on to car straps with ungloved hands. The same don't applies to water closet chains, handles and many other germ holders you will call to your mind.

In studying the peculiar habits of girls I watched a group in the "Ladies' Hat Rooms" at a theater. They took off their hats after much pulling of big daggers—beg pardon, I mean pins—out of hair and hats. These dag—pins, were all promiscuously laid upon a dressing table covered with germ-laden dust, only to be taken up again and held in the mouth. The same process was gone through with when they again put on their hats. Pin after pin was taken from the germ cloth and put in their mouths while they adjusted the angle of their hats.

"Say, Mame, lend me a pin, will you? I've lost one." So out of Mame's mouth came a pin, which was immediately put between the lips of the borrowing girl.

Nasty? Of course. Dangerous? Frightfully so.

Don't put pencils, pins, string and other articles of the kind in your mouths. Why does a girl think her mouth is a receptacle for every little thing she wants to use temporarily?

I have seen girls and women step up to a box office and as soon as the ticket seller had shoved, with his bare hands, a ticket or two through the window, immediately grab up those dangerous pieces of pasteboard and place them between their lips and hold them there until they passed down the line and into the theater.

And probably, shortly after, this same girl or woman will wonder why she has pimples, blotches or sore lips. Then she goes to the druggist for a "face balm" which temporarily hides the real trouble. Finally she has to go to the doctor, who finds it is too late to repair all the damage done through ignorance, foolishness and the drug.

Don't use arsenic in any form for your complexion or to give your face a plump appearance. Some of you will tell me of a girl you know who has a nice plump face from the use of arsenic wafers. "She used 'to be a fright'; skinny in the face and deep lines." Certainly, and now she looks to be in good health.

But she is not; she is in a dangerous state, and if she keeps up the arsenic poisoning she will discover this fact.

In the girl, arsenic will produce a certain amount of fat—unnatural of course—in hollows or pits which full growth will attend to if the girl will have patience. Poisoning herself with arsenic makes fat in the undeveloped tissues of the face. This gives her a plump appearance. So will plenty of whisky, and in about the same manner. But if the fatness was confined only to the cheeks the harm would not be so great, but like whisky again, it puts fat around delicate internal tissues. A girl who has plump cheeks from the use of arsenic has also a "plumpness" around her kidneys, fat over her growing ovaries and inmeshing the tiny cells of the liver. Fatty degeneration of these organs takes place for which there is no remedy.

All headache medicines, such as antipyrine, are not only dangerous, but will ruin a complexion; bring out pimples as certain as the sun shines. The habitual taking of any kind of bromide, bromo seltzer, bromo quinine, and all the other kinds of advertised "sedatives," will cause a peculiar rash not only upon the face, but upon the body. I frequently see girls in shops, stores and even in the high schools, whose faces tell the story of some kind of drug-store "treatment."

Lately there has come to the surface another kind of patent medicine fake which is apt to fool the most open-eyed. This is one you all know of but not about. It is that kind of advertisement which has nothing to sell. It purports to be the outpouring of some philanthropist's heart who wishes to do something for his suffering fellow man—or generally woman. You see he has nothing to sell—don't want your money, simply spend thousands of dollars every week to tell you how to get rid of "that uncomfortable feeling." No matter what is the trouble—house care, worry over your studies or "who sent me THAT valentine"—liver, womb or rheumatism—it is all the same; just go to your druggist and get these simple remedies and take as directed.

Then follows the prescription. At first glance, yes, at the second, you or your mother read the simple home remedies such as tinct. rhubarb, olive oil, simple syrup, extract of quassia, etc., and think that such a recipe must be harmless and certainly good. The advertisement tells you just to get your druggist to fill the recipe. Well, how can there be anything wrong with such harmless and free advice? But you will see inserted among all these harmless and simple and well known remedies, some such direction as "two ounces of badum" or "tinct. of fulum, original package." Now you see the nigger in the woodpile. The whole scheme is to get you to purchase the fake "badum." This is distributed among the druggists and when you go to pay the bill you find that the simple prescription is an expensive one. The druggist tells you that the "badum" is a very expensive ingredient. It probably costs the fakers a few cents and is simply sugar of milk or some equally harmless and legally allowed drug.

Don't kiss anyone but your mother and father.

Don't forget that flies are the most dangerous germ carriers we have, and don't buy or eat anything which has been exposed to flies and street dust.

Don't have any pity for the flies or insects—kill them.

Don't be a giggling girl. The practice of giggling will certainly develop those tiny skin muscles in a way to make your face show some kind of distortion.

I remember a young girl who was brought to me for her constant habit of giggling. It had grown into a habit and really looked like a case of hysteria. But because I told her mother it was a form of hysteria and should be treated as such, she became offended and took the girl elsewhere. I saw the girl, or rather woman, when she was twenty-four years of age, and recognized her by the peculiar conformation of her face. It was the face of a girl giggler. Her facial muscles had become so developed by her uncontrolled girlish habit that nothing could be done for her. I felt sorry for the young woman, for she had grown to be a very charming and estimable one, who was constantly embarrassed by an expression of contempt.

Good laughter, a hilariousness which has for its cause a real sense of humor, is beneficial to everyone. Such expression of humor gives motility to the face and develops a pleasing appearance.

Don't swagger around in public nor attempt to thrust yourself forward. A modest girl will not let herself become prominent in public places. Dressing, acting or talking in any way to attract undue attention will soon ruin a girl's reputation.

Now a little about corsets and a good, supple and attractive figure. I have no objections to corsets as corsets, but every physician knows only too well that a growing girl is injured beyond repair if she, at the developing stage of her life, compresses in any manner the internal organs. Really, this is about all there is to this corset question. If a woman has reached full development with lungs, ovaries, kidneys, all the pelvic organs, having had full play and room for their growth, the proper wearing of corsets will not do her harm; nay, they will do more, they will be a source of comfort to her. Moreover, such a woman will not lace too tightly because always having had full play of her lungs and other internal organs, she will be distressed if they are too tightly confined—their own needs and development send her warning when she has gone too far.

But it is sadly different with the young girl who has from fourteen years or even from sixteen years of age, worn corsets made for the full-grown woman. Every inch of a girl's waist, all the region of the pelvis and the upper portion of her body, should be absolutely free from any pressure. Just take a little growing twig and tie a string around it. Next year you will see a deep constriction. The following years you will notice that the twig does not grow well, that the sap cannot run freely up, that when it does blossom, the blossoms are poorly nourished and lack the luster of its unconstricted companions.

Dress so that there is no pressure upon the pelvis or around the lungs. Try, when you have on one of these modern coats of armor now made for the fat or thin woman, the deep breathing exercises I have recommended. You cannot go through with the exercise.

Oh, but you say, we take off those corsets when we take the exercises. Certainly, but when you gird yourself up again and squeeze, punch and groan while getting into one of those "can't sit down" things, you are undoing all the good the exercises have done.

Let your clothes hang from the shoulders. Shoulders were made to carry weights, the waist and the pelvis to carry and protect the greatest force in nature—the power of motherhood.

If you knew that when you grew to full development you would have to be a carrier of wood or water upon your shoulders, that this would have to be your career, would you go to work and place some constriction or in some way injure the growth of your shoulders—do something which would prevent you from doing what you were born to do?

Of course not. Well then, take the best care of your pelvis and their contents. Give them exercise, shape, health, beauty, by letting them grow unrestricted. You may not know it; but the condition of a woman's pelvis tells in her face. Broad hips mean happy and painless motherhood. Early constriction of the lungs and internal organs means a miserable existence for a woman, married or single.

Early constriction of the body means lack of bust development. This means that your little baby, so hungry for its mother's milk, will have to be artificially fed.

Don't think that there is any other way of a complete bust development than freedom of bodily action while growing. Those advertised things are more than useless; they are positively injurious. You can never have the ability to nurse your child if you fall into the hands of these criminal advertisers of "bust developers."

I have now outlined in a cursory manner the main facts in modern physiology, which, if you allow to sink into your memory, will make for a life of perfect health. Don't think that life is all pleasure or all misery. It is a happy combination. Happy because all our burdens are for a purpose, and when these purposes are well understood, the burdens cease to be real burdens, but tasks whose outcomes are seen to be pleasure.

The real reasons for so much misery among girls and women is unhealth, rather than ill health. Unhealth is avoidable; so is much ill health. You all know how and why.

I have said little to you about morals because when a girl is in perfect health she is moral. By this I mean, perfect mental health, as well as purely physical.

Let me explain. A girl has good physical health, she is also in good mental health, hence she is morally healthy. She has had good home instruction—but not as thorough as is now needed—and has no uncontrollable evil thoughts. Some of her companions tease her upon her moral nicety. One day, with a party, she is persuaded to take a glass of beer or champagne. She takes another. Well; she loses her chastity. Bad girl, immoral girl? Not a bit of it. She fell because she was not MENTALLY in good health. What injured her mentally? The beer and champagne. They will do it every time.

Don't touch them!

Don't think that you know more than your mother about what is best for you. You don't.

Printed by Libri Plureos GmbH in Hamburg,
Germany